Gender and Disability

Women's experiences in the Middle East

Lina Abu-Habib

Oxfam
(UK and Ireland)

Cover photograph: Chris Johnson/Oxfam

First published by Oxfam UK and ireland in 1997
This edition transferred to print-on-demand in 2007

© Oxfam (UK and Ireland) 1997

ISBN 978 0 85598 363 9

A catalogue record for this publication is available from the British Library.

Available from:
Bournemouth English Book Centre, PO Box 1496, Parkstone, Dorset, BH12 3YD, UK
tel: +44 (0)1202 712933; fax: +44 (0)1202 712930; email: oxfam@bebc.co.uk

USA: Stylus Publishing LLC, PO Box 605, Herndon, VA 20172-0605, USA
tel: +1 (0)703 661 1581; fax: +1 (0)703 661 1547; email: styluspub@aol.co

For details of local agents and representatives in other countries, consult our website:
http://www.oxfam.org.uk/publications.html
or contact Oxfam Publishing, Oxfam House, John Smith Drive, Cowley, Oxford, OX4 2JY, UK
tel +44 (0) 1865 472255; fax (0) 1865 472393; email: publish@oxfam.org.uk

Our website contains a fully searchable database of all our titles, and facilities for secure on-line ordering.

Published by Oxfam GB, Oxfam House, John Smith Drive, Cowley, Oxford, OX4 2JY, UK

Oxfam GB is a registered charity, no. 202918, and is a member of Oxfam International.

Contents

Acknowledgments

The material for this book was mostly collected between December 1994 and April 1996 whilst I was on secondment from Oxfam (UKI) Lebanon Office to the Gender Team in Oxford. This intense learning period provided a unique opportunity for research and reflection on programme impact and ways to improve the quality of Oxfam's intervention with poor and vulnerable people notably women with disabilities. It was possible for me to do this work because of the support and encouragement of a number of people and colleagues. Much appreciation goes to Ernst Ligteringen, then Oxfam (UKI) Asia Director for fully supporting this initiative, which was a new way of working within Oxfam. I also wish to thank Dr. Maitrayee Mukhopadhyay, then Oxfam (UKI) Gender Advisor for Asia and the Middle East, for her invaluable guidance, for sharing her wide and rich knowledge and making this experience so worthwhile. Most of all, I would like to thank my partner and closest colleague, Omar Traboulsi, Oxfam's Middle East/Maghreb Regional Representative for his constant support, advice and encouragement in seeing this work through.

Last but not least, my thanks goes to all the women and men with disabilities whom I have interviewed and who have shared with me their intimate experiences, frustrations, and aspirations. I sincerely hope that this book will contribute to furthering their cause.

Lina Abu-Habib
Beirut, July 1997

This young woman never left her house before she met the Lebanese Sitting Handicapped Association (LHSA). LHSA built a ramp to make her house in Byblos, Lebanon accessible.

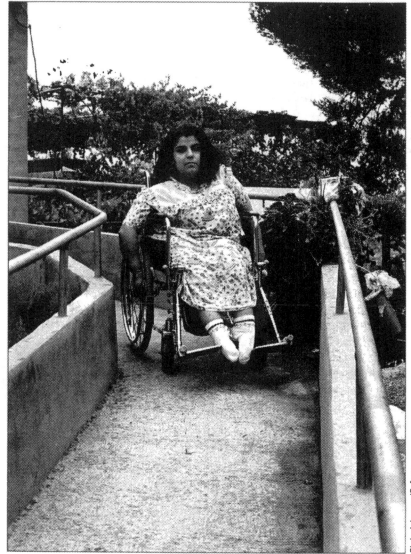

Chris Johnson/Oxfam

1

Introduction

There is clearly a conflict between feminism's rhetoric of inclusion and failure to include disability. (Sherr 1992)

Shortly after Canadian feminist film-maker Bonnie Sherr suffered a stroke which left her disabled and wheelchair bound, she wrote that she felt abandoned by feminism. As articles in this book assert, in the Middle East, as in other parts of the world, such as India, for example, disabled women have not been fully integrated in either the disability movement or the women's movement.

Due attention and consideration needs to be given to the gender aspect of disability and how this serves as a main factor in determining the meaning and implication of disability, and its perception by the non-disabled world. When I asked a professional woman, who works for a major international development agency in the Middle East, about references for this introduction, she retorted spontaneously: 'so, now you're hunting for gender in disability also... isn't this a superfluous academic exercise?' For me, this comment epitomises the failure of feminists, and activists in the disability movement, to make the links between gender and disability, as two aspects of social identity which lead to potential marginalisation from a society which is designed and run by able-bodied men.

The relatively few statistics which exist on disabled women provide unquestionable confirmation of a fact which is very obvious to gender and development workers who work with disabled women: it is necessary and relevant to research and work on issues of gender and disability, because disabled women are indeed worse off than their able-bodied sisters.

To give a few instances: women with disabilities are twice as prone to divorce, separation, and violence than able-bodied women (UNDP 1995). A higher prevalence of disability amongst boys has been noted in several studies from Yemen and Egypt (Dr. Azzah Ghanem, University of Sanaa', 1993 — *Women with Disability in Egypt,* unpublished paper presented to the ME seminar on 'The roles of the family in integrating disabled women into society', Amman, 1994). Researchers have attributed this to a concurrently higher mortality among girls because of lack of adequate care to disabled girls. Finally, in India, the Blind Men Association, a major rehabilitation association for blind and visually impaired persons in Ahmedabad, attributes the visibly higher rate of blindness amongst rural women to a similar cause: women with cataract and other eye diseases are far less likely than men to be transported to the city to have the necessary surgical operation and treatment (personal communication, BMA/Ahmedabad, July 1995).

A microcosm of development

Following arguments about the marginalisation of disabled people from development (Coleridge 1993), and how this is reminiscent of the marginalisation of Southern countries from economic wealth-creation, it could be argued that the situation of disabled women in 1996 can be seen as a microcosm of the problems of marginalisation of many groups of people from decision-making, social life, and economic development.

In 1995, I was involved in a research project for Oxfam in the Middle East (Lebanon, Egypt, and Yemen) and India, which had as its objective to identify the interaction between gender and disability, in order to improve programme planning and policy making. When I started preparing for the research project, I found that it was extremely difficult to find any literature which looked simultaneously at women, gender issues, disability, and the Middle East. The dearth of studies and research on this subject, whilst general literature on disability in the region abounds, simultaneously shows the invisibility of disabled women in our communities, and a corresponding lack of interest in this topic on the part of local and international researchers.

The literature which has just recently started to appear on gender and disability is often characterised by stress on the 'double disability' of disabled women. Disabled women are indeed doubly marginalised by their communities, and by organisations at national and international level. At international level, this is reflected in the fact that in 1981, the UN Decade for the Disabled was launched, overlapping with the UN Decade for Women for its first four years. Yet neither Decade seems to have evoked much interest in the particular situation of women with disabilities.

Welfare, rights, and the disability movement

Just as men assume that they know what women want, so non-disabled assume that they know what disabled people want. (Hannaford, 1985)

Worldwide, men and women with disabilities have relatively better life-chances today than a decade or more ago. For one thing, disability has come out into the open. Disabled persons have fought the practice of incarceration in residential homes and hospitals, a 'treatment' which was legitimate not only in the Middle East but also in the Western world (Finkelstein, 1991).

There is a sense among the able-bodied that disabled people need their protection. Concern with the welfare of disabled people is seen as 'charitable'. Yet these breakthroughs can only partially be attributed to a change of heart on the part of the able-bodied decision-makers at national and international level. As Lambert puts it, 'my survival at every level depends on maintaining good relationships with able-bodied people' (Lambert 1989, 39).

Achievements and successes in advocacy work on disability can be attributed in large measure to the efforts and perseverance of groups of disabled people. The disability movement is, in many countries of the Middle East, pro-active, strong, and involved in advocacy on the rights of the disabled. Disabled activists from various parts of the Middle East have become more vocal on essential issues such as rights for disabled persons, representation, and full integration and independence. Fifteen years ago, such initiatives were in their infancy. Even now, such successes remain small-scale in comparison to the need, and possible only when lobbying groups have gained strength and negotiating power, and receive the good-will and cooperation of the public.

If certain policy changes have in fact occurred, changes in discriminatory perceptions, attitudes, and behaviour have been far slower. Ensuring rights for the disabled does not in itself affect the prevailing patriarchal system, and therefore is not threatening. In addition, politicians can always postpone commitments by using the all-too-common excuses of financial constraints, conflicting priorities, and the fact that isolation and discrimination can only be attributed to mere ignorance.

Thus, the strong message from the non-disabled world remains that the lives of disabled persons are not necessarily worth living. Both men and women with disabilities are made to feel 'different'; they fail to conform to a traditionally and socially agreed norm of beauty and strength. Pity, condescension, embarrassment, or a mixture of the three, are the reactions most commonly encountered by men and women who have a disability, from non-disabled people. Many activists believe that

3

disabled people are in some senses considered by able-bodied people —
both women and men — to be less than human (Morris, 1993).

*During the summer of 1993, there was a major Israeli military offensive in South
Lebanon which caused hundreds of casualties and massive exodus and
displacement. The Lebanese Sitting Handicapped Association (LSHA), along
with other local NGOs, was involved in relief and emergency work. LSHA was
surveying damages suffered by disabled persons and their families, as well as
cases of new injuries. On arriving in the village of Kfarroumane, they asked as
usual for the co-operation of the villagers in surveying the houses. Knowing that
LSHA is an association of disabled persons, a woman approached them and told
them that she knew of a next-door neighbour who had a disabled daughter, now
a teenager. However, she had not seen her for a long time, and certainly not after
the military offensive. She was concerned because their house had been directly
hit by a mortar shell. On entering the half-destroyed house, LSHA volunteers
discovered the girl inside, injured and in a pitiful state. An investigation
revealed that when the family fled the village, her father refused to take her,
leaving her under fire and perhaps hoping that she would be killed, and this
would be 'God's wish'. He also told LSHA volunteers that he had preferred to
save their cow because she is more useful to them than their disabled daughter.
When LSHA wanted to take the girl to a nearby hospital for her wound to be
treated, her father categorically refused. 'What for?" he asked 'So that I start
paying for her?' LSHA had to ask for the assistance of the local gendarmerie to
take the girl to hospital.*

Women and the disability movement

Where disabled lobby groups have been active in advocating changes in
discriminatory laws, emphasis has not tended to be placed on rendering
this work gender-sensitive. Although lobbying for rights, services,
education, and employment for disabled people in general is of utmost
importance and long overdue, such work is of very limited use to disabled women if they suffer discrimination differently and more deeply
on grounds of their sex.

Disabled women in different contexts have complained that rehabilitation programmes appear to have been designed to suit disabled men's
aspiration for recovering their masculinity and sexuality, while the needs and
aspirations of disabled women are often ignored (Begum, 1992, Morris, 1993).

The leadership of the disability movement is to a large extent still
dominated by disabled men, who may consider their own experience as
the norm. In the case of Lebanon, the country of which I have most
personal knowledge, only one of the current disabled associations is

presided over by a woman (personal communication 1996). However, she has acceded to the post by appointment and following the prolonged sickness of the former male president. At the time of writing this book, there are no disabled women leading or presiding over associations of disabled persons in any other Middle Eastern country.

The disability movement in the Middle East has yet to herald the specific issues pertinent to disabled women on its agenda. Even now, major international disability events which have direct implications for policy making, such as the September 1996 conference on disability convened by the ILO in Sana'a, Yemen, have little input from people who see gender as a central concern for women who are disabled.

Just as statistics on women assume able-bodied status, statistics on disabled people frequently fail to disaggregate by sex the people being studied. Nevertheless, empirical evidence shows beyond doubt that disabled women have had less access than disabled men to the potential benefits that may be gained from national governments and non-governmental organisations set up to address the practical and strategic needs of disabled people.

Disabled women in the feminist movement

If the marginalisation of women within the disability movement is being to some extent addressed and rectified, disabled women remain absent from the leadership and agenda of the women's movement, in the Middle East and beyond. For the past 30 years, since International Women's Year in 1975, the women's movement has struggled to place women's rights and needs in development squarely on the international agenda.

According to the last *Human Development Report* (UNDP, 1995), there have recently been a number of concrete, albeit limited, changes for the better in the lives of women in the Middle East, which is the regional context of the case studies in this book.

The *Report* states that more women have access to basic services such as health and education (UNDP 1995), yet women's strategic interests have yet to be met: women will have to wait longer for full inclusion and better representation in political life. But the main point in respect of the concerns of this book is that there is no evidence that disabled women have benefited either practically or strategically, on equal terms with able-bodied women, from this advancement. How could such evidence exist, when most official statistics and research on women ignore this aspect of social difference?

I attended the Beijing Preparatory Meeting in Amman in November 1994, and by the end of the NGO meeting, I had given up trying to locate a disabled woman amongst the 800 or so participants. This was surprising, because hardly a month before this meeting, a pre-preparatory meeting was convened in the same city, especially for women with disabilities, to discuss strategies to ensure that their perspectives were included in the Beijing process, and in particular at the subsequent Prepcom meeting.

A similar chain of events occurred at other regional Prepcoms for Beijing: for example, in the Prepcom meeting held in Dakar during that same period, disabled women participants strongly criticised the conference organisers in Senegal, for failing to expect and accommodate women with disabilities. According to the participants, none of their major requirements to allow their full participation in the Dakar Prepcom were met: from accessible toilets to transport which was suitable for the use of disabled people.

In parallel with questions asked in the women's movement, the question of representation of one group by another — seen in the feminist movement, and in international development bodies — also arises in the context of disability and gender. It takes outspoken, eloquent, disabled feminists to be able to infiltrate the women's movement, and put forward the disability agenda. Before leaving to attend the UN IV Conference in Beijing, Miriam, a young woman who uses a wheelchair, visited one of the pioneers of the women's movement of Lebanon to inquire about the attitude of her association vis-à-vis women with disabilities. Taken by surprise with an unexpected question, the activist replied 'er... dear, well we're thinking of you all the time...' (personal communication, 1996).

The fact that the representation of disabled women by others is problematic has been apparent even at fora which are intended to discuss their concerns. For example, a seminar on the role of the family in integrating disabled women into society run by ESCWA (United Nations Economic and Social Commission for Western Asia), in Amman, Jordan, in October 1994, and a Conference on Blind Women held by the World Blind Union in Amman in 1995, were both described by many of the participants as events lacking any significant participation of disabled women; the fact that there was virtually no disabled presence meant that there was a consequent lack of focus and clarity on possible strategies for follow-up.

Whatever the difficulties involved in disabled women's participation, the Fourth UN Conference on Women, held in Beijing in 1995, witnessed the highest number of disabled women participants to date — two hundred in total (although the representation from the Middle East was fewer than ten women). This was the first time there had ever been an organised representation of disabled women at an international women's conference. Whilst the conference itself was poorly prepared to receive disabled women and communicate with them effectively, disabled women themselves were well-organised, and demanded that they be listened to. This event showed the importance of the presence and representation of disabled women, in events where policy decisions can often be taken on behalf of disabled women *in absentia*.

Beijing was a landmark for disabled women, who refused to be relegated to a category of 'women with special needs'. Their struggle to be heard as individuals in their own right, and on equal terms with able-bodied women, was reminiscent of the earlier days of the women's movement where women were fighting for the equal rights, and the right to be heard.

Apart from the personal experience of being disabled oneself, women may experience the issue from another perspective, in their role as primary carers for children and other family members, and within the community. This issue, too, is pertinent to the wider concerns of the women's movement. For many years now, feminists have emphasised the value of the work of caring, and questioned the fact that much of this work remains invisible to national and international planners and policy-makers, in development agencies as well as governments.

In the Middle East, as elsewhere, mothers of disabled children are in most instances the sole care givers and nurturers at home, a role they have to fulfil in addition to the already back-breaking household chores and other productive functions (Begum, N, 1992). As carers, women have to spend the rest of their lives at home, nursing the disabled child, and caring for the family as a whole, with no possibility of any improvement later in life. Again, planners have failed to consider this important aspect of disability, and the fact that women carers will forever be unable to care for and invest in themselves. Caring for the disabled will have to be added to the list of other unrecognised and unpaid tasks that women have to perform. As if this were not enough, in the Middle East context, mothers are invariably blamed, shamed, and stigmatised for the birth of a disabled child.

The structure of this book

The next chapter will describe empirical research on gender and disability carried out in the Middle East and India. The research seeks to identify the gender dimensions of disability, and ask how and why disability is experienced differently according to gender. The main findings of this research are categorised according to the different levels of household, community and state.

Chapter 3 consists of case studies written by development workers, and disabled men and women themselves, in different countries of the

Middle East. Each of these personal accounts highlights particular aspects of disability as it affects women and men, but most importantly, the writers examine such experience from a practical perspective, discussing potential and actual strategies for social development work, and placing emphasis on present successes and future challenges.

Some case studies come from organisations set up to address problems faced by disabled people. It is striking that, while gender and disability is looked at from different angles in each of these contributions, there is similarity in how each organisation is experimenting in its work, and trying hard to discover how best to integrate a gender perspective. This struggle sometimes yields a feeling of insecurity, and was so threatening to one of the organisations that it decided to reject the idea of working on gender issues altogether.

Finally, the last chapter of this book concludes by drawing out the main lessons and how these can be integrated into strategies for action. This chapter argues that intervention in the field of disability, as in any other, cannot be successful in producing social change unless the analysis guiding it is gender-aware. It particularly stresses the need to listen to disabled women.

References

Begum, N 'Disabled women and the feminist agenda',
in *Feminist Review*, 1992.

Finkelstein, V 'Disability: an administrative challenge',
in Oliver, M (ed) *Social Work: Disabled People and Disabling Environment* Kingsley: London, 1991.

Hannaford, S *Living Outside Inside*, Canterbury Press: Berkeley, California, 1985.

Lambert, A 'Disability and violence', in *Sinister Wisdom*, 1989.

Morris, J *Pride against Prejudice*, Women's Press, London, 1993.

Morris, J (ed) *Able Lives*, Women's Press: London, 1989.

Sen, A K 'Gender and ccoperation conflicts'in Tinker I
Persistent Inequalities, OUP, 1990.

Sherr, B 'We are who we are: feminism and disability',
in *Ms* November 1992.

UNDP *Human Development Report 1995*, OUP: Oxford, 1995.

2

Working with disabled women: reviewing our approach

In this chapter, I will briefly analyse aspects of disability in relation to gender through discussing the results of a research survey undertaken in 1995 to examine the work of Oxfam on disability in the Middle East and India. The chapter also discusses underlying forms of resistance to addressing the issues raised by gender analysis in the field of disability and development. Finally, it suggests strategies for integrating such a gender analysis in work with disabled people.

The research was carried out in line with our belief that all interventions designed to facilitate social change, carried out by funding agencies and non-governmental organisations (NGOs), ought to be based on a deep understanding of gender relations in a particular context, founded on factual evidence. Oxfam has explicitly worked on gender issues for ten years, and has had an organisational Gender Policy, ratified at the highest levels, since 1993. This formal commitment to working to promote gender equity and the empowerment of women prompted Oxfam in the Middle East to examine the impact of our work on the lives of disabled women.

Sara Longwe, a development consultant from Zambia, has suggested that gender issues 'evaporate' from development programmes (Longwe 1995). One of many justifications given for a failure to highlight the centrality of gender issues in women's and men's lives is lack of time on the part of the researcher or development worker. 'I have specifically asked the consultant to concentrate only on disability and disregard gender because we do not have time...', stated one development programme manager, attempting to justify why a major evaluation of disability work in his programme area had completely failed to take gender issues into account (personal communication, 1995).

As Longwe observed, such excuses are all too common in development programmes, whether these deal with disabled people, refugees, fishing communities, farmers, or other 'vulnerable' groups. As many gender and development researchers and practitioners have observed over the past two decades, the result has invariably been to further marginalise women away from the development process and reinforce their inferior position in private and public life. The truth of the matter is that unless there is will, commitment, and in-depth understanding, no time will ever be found for 'doing gender'.

Our findings showed telling examples of the profound isolation of women who are disabled, and the neglect of their needs, aspirations, and interests. Their social isolation as women is deepened by their disabled status (Boylan 1991).

The evolution of Oxfam's work on disability in the region

In line with the trends outlined in the introduction to this book, Oxfam's work on issues relating to disability in the Middle East has changed considerably during the last two decades. First, Oxfam's agenda has been influenced by developments in the wider movement of individuals and organisations which are working on disability. Over this period, disabled people have become more organised, taking a proactive role and rather than merely remaining recipients of aid, stepping into the public arena to discuss injustice and discrimination and their root causes. For example, associations were formed in Egypt in the early 1990s by parents of children with learning disabilities, to undertake general awareness-raising activities in addition to lobbying and advocacy. In the case of Lebanon, the first organisation of disabled persons with a clear rights and advocacy agenda was formed during the war in 1981, to be followed by several similar organisations, including a group calling itself the National Association for the Rights of Disabled Persons. Disabled people in other Arab countries started to organise in the late 1980s, and many of them made links with the Lebanese organisations. These groups brought with them a new agenda which stressed representation and full integration, and demanded to be heard not only by the authorities but also by foreign agencies such as Oxfam. In addition, Oxfam's own analysis has changed over the years, affecting its ways of working on development issues with counterpart organisations.

Changing thinking on disability

For many years, and within the NGO circle, thinking on, and discussions of, disability were centred on 'models' which characterised ways of thinking about disability as an issue. On the one hand, a 'medical' model, which focused on the physical and mental characteristics of disability, was dismissed as 'bad' — in the belief that this was static, reductive, and exploited disabled people. At the other extreme was the 'social' model of disability, which emphasised that it is not the physical or mental condition itself which disadvantages disabled people, but the social context which is designed by and for able-bodied people, thus discriminating against those whose bodily functions differ from the norm. The difference between the models was clear-cut and easy to comprehend. The social model was embraced as useful and progressive, and provided the springboard for Oxfam's initial involvement in supporting the 'disability movement' in the Middle East.

Despite the fact that the basic rationale for Oxfam's support was a genuine solidarity with a group characterised by being 'vulnerable', 'marginalised', 'oppressed', 'poorly-represented', and 'impoverished', this is actually an over-simplification of a complex state of affairs. For example, one assumption behind Oxfam's strategy of alliance and partnership based on solidarity was that 'the disabled' form a cohesive and homogeneous group, working towards a clear and shared goal, and motivated by similar interests.

Understanding the links between disability and gender

In the early days of working on disability issues, it became obvious to field staff who maintain close, almost day-to-day contacts with counterparts, that the disability world, in common with any other, is fraught with power struggles. We soon saw that we needed to consciously reject simplistic analyses which focus on disability in isolation from other important issues and social relations. Most importantly, we recognised that disabled people are not sexless: they are men and women with different interests, different characteristics including age, economic status, aspirations, and different life-experiences.

The assumption that the disability movement represents *all* disabled people, and shares the fruits of its successes equally, was proved wrong. It is often argued that it is not necessary to integrate a women's rights perspective with that of disabled people's rights, in that disabled men and women are equal already. There is a parallel here with the assumption that increased family income will benefit all family or household members equally (Kabeer 1994 challenges this view).

In practice, the argument may go as follows: 'Our association treats disabled men and women equally. For example, we have always responded positively to women seeking business loans from our credit programme. It is not our fault if only two of the eighteen applicants are women.'

11

A statement like this makes one wonder how disabled men and women can possibly be said to be equal, in a social, economic, and political context where non-disabled women and men are obviously unequal. Is it to imply that disabled women and men are gender-neutral beings, without the interests and needs dictated by gender identity?

In fact, such statements in themselves provide tangible proof of inequality between the sexes. Our investigation confirms this, indicating that although associations or individuals may respond similarly to disabled men and women, they often overlook the fact that inequality starts in babyhood. This may explain why far fewer disabled women than men have acquired the education, skill, and confidence needed to apply for a business loan.

'Weakening' the focus

Another set of objections to addressing gender issues is concerned with a fear that taking on a gender perspective will somehow 'weaken' the search for social justice for the disabled.

A disabled man responded to a female colleague who proposed that their association should look at the specific predicament of women with disabilities as follows: 'we are all fighting for the same cause, so let us close ranks ... it is not enough that we are weak as it is, now you want to divide the movement into men and women...' (personal experience, 1995). The philosophy here appears to be that women and men should unite to fight discrimination against, and marginalisation of, disabled people. Once this fight is won, then they can start looking at 'secondary' issues such as that of women with disabilities. In this light, the plight of the population in question is so great that introducing a new 'problem' will inevitably lead to scattering already meagre resources and distracting attention from the main cause (Abu Habib 1995).

This argument is reminiscent of arguments advanced in situations where class or racial oppression is seen by many as the sole, all-encompassing problem. In the Middle Eastern context, parallels can be found in debates on the early struggles for national independence in most countries of the Middle East. In fact, women who participated actively and wholeheartedly in liberation movements, subsuming their interests as women, have seen those interests deprioritised (and in some cases ignored altogether) once liberation was achieved (Daoud, 1993).

In the case of disability, there is a long way to go before the aspired-to state of total equality and non-discrimination is achieved. Given this fact, there is a risk that working for the cause of women with disabilities will be postponed indefinitely.

Changing ways of working on disability

While Oxfam's work in the 1970s typically took the form of financial support to large rehabilitation institutions which worked with people with many different disabilities, Oxfam now supports associations of disabled persons engaged primarily in advocacy and lobbying in several countries of the region: Lebanon, Palestinian Territories, Yemen, and Jordan. At the time of writing, Oxfam is supporting capacity-building, networking, advocacy, and the provision of alternative services, such as the integration of blind children in mainstream schooling, or subsidised and accessible transportation for disabled students and employees. As well as being valuable in themselves, such initiatives are in the nature of pilot projects, to illustrate and support the advocacy work of the disability associations. A close relationship, involving funding and other support, is maintained with selected rehabilitation associations, who hold an important role in training, curriculum-development, and expert consultancy at both the local and regional levels.

A deaf woman, a speech therapist at the School for the Deaf,
Salt, Jordan, practising signing.

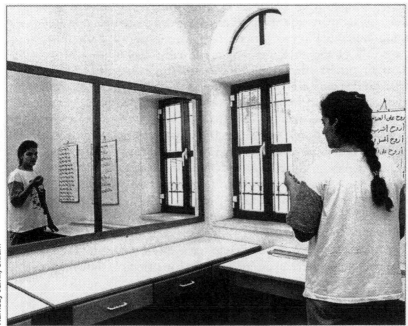

Ramsay Jamil/Oxfam

Challenging internalised assumptions

As can be seen from the above, it is imperative to disaggregate the category of 'the disabled'. Not only is this a misleading, monolithic term which implies that every disabled person, and all disabilities, are the same, but it also categorises people by one aspect of their identity in a way which is likely to lead to social prejudice against them.

In most of the literature dealing with the experience of disability experienced, little differentiation is made between men and women. Yet there is now ample proof, in addition to the findings of this study, that disability is experienced differently according to gender. Physical, social, psychological, and other disadvantages caused by disability have indeed a strong gender dimension. Coping mechanisms developed by disabled persons and their family are also gender-differentiated.

There can be little value in adopting a blanket, standardised approach to disability, because the individual experience of disability varies markedly by sex and according to other important factors such as age — and also, of course, the nature of the disability.

Listening to disabled women

Oxfam staff in the Middle East began to build a better understanding of the lives of disabled women through working with them daily, and listening to what they were saying. It was very clear that we needed to review many of the initial assumptions described above. Rather than undertaking a typical evaluation, we carried out a small, qualitative study of the situation of women with disabilities. This sort of research is most effective in showing telling examples, and suggesting likely trends, but it cannot be, and is not intended to be, statistically valid. A total of 18 women and five men with disabilities, of different ages and socio-economic background, were interviewed using a structured open-ended questionnaire. Respondents were asked about the history of their disability, their recollection of early experiences of discrimination, their carer and the decision-makers in their lives, and the resources made available to them. Interviewees were selected from Lebanon, Yemen, and Egypt. For the sake of comparison, seven interviews with women with disabilities were undertaken in India as well.

Although there was no particular focus on the type of disability, the respondents selected had disabilities which in principle should not make it impossible for them to lead an independent life.

Testing assumptions

The research study started from a basic assumption that the situation of disabled women and men is different, with disabled women having to deal with additional discrimination because of their gender. This discrimination is believed to have its roots in the household, where decisions about the initial allocation of tangible and intangible resources is made. This stage is thought to be important because access to these resources will largely determine the future of a disabled person.

We were therefore interested in identifying who takes decisions on behalf of the disabled person in a household. What are the perceptions of this decision-maker as to the life-chances of the disabled person? Does this perception vary according to the gender of the disabled person? Finally, how are resources allocated according to these perceptions? In short, the study aimed at measuring resource allocation for the disabled against perceptions of the decision-maker in the household. The main interviewees were the disabled themselves. We did not often speak to parents directly, though in many instances they were present during the interview, and intervened at different stages.

Our main assumption was that decisions regarding disabled persons in their early lives, made by older family members, are highly influenced by the decision-maker's perception of the life-chances of the disabled person, which in turn is coloured by the disabled person's sex.

Decision-making and disability

The role of fathers in the lives of a child with disability appeared to be all-powerful. All respondents who were disabled since their childhood reported that, although they were physically cared for by their mothers, it was their fathers who decided about important matters such as medical treatment, education and training, and, in the case of girls, going out of the house.

Disabled men, who are not household heads, may take on the responsibility for family decision-making in some circumstances, for example, if the household head is himself affected by age or infirmity. This happened in the case of Samir, a young man with polio, who is the eldest son in a family of six. He has two sisters with learning disabilities. Samir's father is now elderly, and has delegated decisions on family matters to him.

I am the oldest in my family. My father trusts me with family responsibilities. He had me undergo any possible surgical operation to cure my polio condition and

helped me to finish technical school. He always believed in me. I now operate a
taxi in addition to my paid job in the Ministry. My mother took care of me when
I was little. She now takes care of my two younger sisters, who have learning
disabilities. However, it is I who decide on what to do with them. They respect me
and fear me, otherwise we would have chaos.

Factors in decision-making

When money is in short supply, decisions must be taken on which child,
or children, in the family to educate. Education may not be perceived as
a priority for girls, and having a disability makes it even less likely that a
girl will be educated. Yet decision-making on educating women is not
only influenced by financial considerations, but by social and cultural
norms, and by intangible factors such as particular affection between
family members. A main rationale for education is to fit children to find
employment. It can, therefore, be argued that it is rational that, when
resources are limited, families should choose to educate able-bodied
children rather than disabled children, and boys rather than girls.

In general, the majority of women respondents who were disabled
and living in poverty reported a high degree of scepticism from their ·
families, (and in particular from their fathers) as to their future life
chances, and the potential for them to lead a fulfilling and independent
life. This scepticism meant that very few resources tended to be made
available to these women early in their lives. They had received little
education and as a result, their chances of achieving any form of
economic or social independence were very low. In contrast, the disabled
men we interviewed were to a large extent supported by their family
and, at the time of the interview, they were all involved in paid jobs, in
either the private or the public sectors.

Yet we found that it is not necessarily the case that disabled women are
unable to find employment. For example, some disabled women involved
in our research came from well-to-do socio-economic backgrounds, and
after receiving education had subsequently become gainfully employed
or set up their own businesses. Disabled women coming from wealthy
families may not only have the chance to be educated, but may also be
able to obtain medical treatment in Europe, or study abroad.

Madiha, from Yemen, finds that being disabled can even bring certain
compensations:

I know that this sounds strange, but being a disabled woman has given me
certain privileges that I would have never dreamt of had I been an able-bodied
Yemeni woman. I go out from my house on my own, and take a taxi to go to work.

I make my own money. I participate in many public events and meet with my male colleagues on a daily basis. My able-bodied sisters are not allowed to do any of this. I guess my parents are not afraid for my safety and honour. They probably think: 'She is disabled, who in the world would want anything to do with her'.

Aisha, an Egyptian architect who had lived for years in the UK, reported being indulged by her father. She was the preferred child. In fact, when presenting his two daughters to visitors, her father used to say '..this is my pretty daughter (the able bodied daughter) and this my intelligent daughter (Aisha)...' The example of Aisha shows clearly the role of intangibles such as emotion and preference in influencing decisions; confirming that it is reductive to focus only on economic considerations (Sen 1990).

This appeared to be the case even in families where economic concerns might have been expected to be over-riding, as well as in wealthy families. For instance, a disabled girl from a very poor urban slum in Cairo attributed her education to the fact that she was the only member of the family to have won the affection of her father.

My father was a very violent man. He used to brutalise my mother, and all my brothers and sisters. It is strange, but I am the only one with whom he was kind and loving. He encouraged me to go to school and learn a trade.

Social networks, relationships, and marriage

Discussions about friendship and marriage were perhaps the most interest-ing parts of the interviews we conducted during our research, though these were often the hardest issues to address. For instance, the topic of marriage tended to bring up issues like sexual relationships and intimate aspects of marital relationships, which caused embarrassment to respondents, particularly when the interviewee was a woman. Men were less inhibited in talking about marriage and, implicitly, sexual relations.

Very few disabled women respondents, or disabled women known to our respondents, had married. While, in general, most disabled men did not consider that their ability to become husbands was affected by their disability (it should be noted, however, that most of the men who were interviewed had disabilities which would not necessarily affect their reproductive functions, and this aspect was not addressed in the inter-views), women's marriage chances are profoundly affected by disability

Hiba Hagrass, from Cairo, Egypt, explains the prevailing attitude:

You have to realise that men and women are judged using completely different criteria. A man should be strong, able to earn money and provide for his family.

Many disabled men, regardless of the type of their disability, can fit this description. A woman is judged according to a completely different scale. She need not be clever. In fact, this may be a liability. She should be beautiful and attractive, a good housekeeper able to comply with the demands of her husband, particularly physical ones. A disabled woman cannot be beautiful, not when judged according to our scale of beauty, in any case. And a disabled woman cannot certainly be sexually attractive! Is there anything left on the list of requirements after that?

Where disabled women do marry, our research indicated that they may have to make numerous concessions. Sewa, an Indian woman from a very wealthy family, who has a motor disability, married Paresh, a blind man who, before their marriage, was not involved in any development or community work. Sewa, herself the Vice-President of a major association of disabled people, introduced her husband to the world of NGOs, and found him a job. Paresh climbed the social ladder aided by his wife's connections, and developed a wide network of relationships. He was particularly popular with his contacts in overseas development agencies.

However, Paresh soon became bored with his disabled wife. He had many potential partners to choose from among his new contacts, and had several extra-marital affairs. His being blind did not seem to affect his popularity or physical attraction. 'He used to humiliate me in public, and undermine my work and my personal interests' says Sewa. She appeared to us to be using his disability as a reason for placing the blame for infidelity on the women rather than her husband:

Although my parents became fed-up with him, I used to understand that he only did this because he could not cope with his own disability. It is not really his fault if he took other women. I always say it's the women's fault. How could they do this, when they know he is married?

Male respondents, in contrast, considered that as long as they were able to 'provide for' their wives, they were perfectly eligible for marriage and parenthood. One particularly significant interview involved a very heated group discussion with two women and three men from one of the disabled groups in Lebanon. Although the discussion was on disability and marriage, it took an interesting turn to focus on what are the 'agreed' roles of men and women.

Hassan, a young man who had recently gained employment as a computer operator at the Ministry of Electricity, told us that he is engaged to Hind. He has polio and uses crutches. She is able-bodied. They are planning to elope, because Hind will not tell her parents of her intention to marry Hassan. She is sure that they will categorically refuse

Chris Johnson/Oxfam

Disabled women are far less likely to marry than are disabled men. Samar, a founding member of the LHSA, is one of the very few women with physical disabilities to have married in Lebanon. She lives with her husband, who has also been affected by polio, and their two able-bodied children.

her marriage to a disabled man. Hassan's family has no problems with the whole idea. Neither does he. He has a permanent job in the public sector and makes extra money doing odd jobs. In addition, he told us, 'I can give her what she wants, everything she wants'. The insinuation here was clearly about sexual relations.

Continuing on the same topic of marriage and sex, Hassan added that he is 'totally against the idea of marriage for disabled woman'. When we asked him why, he retorted that a disabled woman 'can never satisfy her husband's needs: this is not just about physical needs but also house-keeping. How on earth do you expect her to maintain the house and keep it clean?'.

We asked him if his views would change if the wife was able to employ domestic help, or if her disability was such that she could manage most of the housekeeping.

Well, maybe. But with age, her health will deteriorate faster than an able-bodied woman, especially if she bears children. She could never raise children properly. Why, her husband would be having to spend time caring for her. Who would want to do that?

Hassan's tirade took place in front of Fadwa, who is a disabled colleague of his, and who is about to marry a disabled man. She appeared to be unconsciously or consciously refraining from joining in the conversation. Her disabled fiance was also present at the interview, and did not say anything either.

The position of Abdallah, the former president of this association, was most interesting. Despite the fact that Abdallah stated that 'as a matter of principle, I stand for the marriage of men and women with disabilities', he contradicted himself immediately in the same interview:

We need to challenge these taboos and social stigmas within our society. But if we want to be practical, we have to admit that only men with disabilities should marry. Disabled women will never be able to be 'complete' partners to any man.

Social networks

Not only does gender identity affect access to resources within the household, but also at the wider community level. Most women interviewed mentioned that whereas disabled men may become key figures in their society, commanding respect and admired for their courage and achievement, it was far more difficult for disabled women to gain social recognition. In line with this, for most of the disabled women living in poverty to whom we spoke, it was difficult to find and maintain social networks. It is important, though, to stress that economic status is closely linked to gender and the two are joint determining factors: disabled men and well-off disabled women did not seem to have any significant difficulty in participating in community affairs and social life. This was especially true of those we interviewed who were employed, who had developed a circle of friends over the course of their careers.

However, the situation of one young woman we interviewed was in marked contrast to this general picture. She had received a serious leg injury during the war, and had to leave school as a result. She was the only disabled young girl from a poor background who seemed to be leading an active social life. We discovered during the interview that her father had been dead for years, thus leaving her mother with full respon-sibility and decision-making power. The mother interrupted the inter-view to say:

I do not like to see her hanging around in the house. I like her to go the beach and to parties with her friends. I wish I could convince her to go back to school, but after all, it is her own decision.

Our research into disabled people's access to community life and social networks thus confirmed findings of an earlier study undertaken in Palestine with six disabled women (Awdeh and alHajj, 1992). This study showed that men who had become disabled during the Intifada had become local heroes, hailed by their communities. This was not the case for women, regardless of the cause of their disabilities, which in many cases was conflict-related.

Implications of the research for Oxfam's work

The way in which disability is experienced is profoundly affected and determined by gender. Where a disability has served to block the chances of a fulfilling life for a woman, the same did not seem to happen in the case of men. Gender ideology can be seen to permeate all aspects of life, and determines power relations in the form of social hierarchies, attitudes, and the distribution of resources within households and at community level. Gender considerations are as pertinent to the experi-ences of disabled people as they are to those who are able-bodied, yet they may be overlooked because the disability may be the most obvious factor influencing social identity. Gender issues are thus harder to address in this group, since gender differentiation is less visible than among non-disabled people. In fact, disability should be understood as actually reinforcing inequalities between men and women. This is powerfully illustrated by the experience of Zeinab, from Lebanon:

I had polio when I was very young. My parents were told that I would never be able to walk normally again. My mother struggled so that I could have as many surgical operations as possible, but she never let me go to school. In the institutions where I was staying, all the other girls were going to school except me. My mother said it was not important for me to learn. I am now 26 years old, and totally illiterate. I learned to sew, and I have been working in sewing factories for ten years. My mother and father do not work, and my brother is unemployed. My father gave him his shop, to start his own business, but somehow, he managed to lose everything. He only comes home to ask for money, which he spends on alcohol, and other things. Despite all this, my parents love and respect him and dare not confront him. I, on the other hand, am not allowed to go out except to go to work. They have forbidden me to participate in a summer camp for disabled people. They have even stopped me from marrying a man that I was in love with. They said that even if I eloped, they'd find me and kill me. They could do that! I got scared and left the man I was involved with. My parents say that I am disabled and cannot marry. But that is not true. They do not want me to leave home because my salary is their only income. Sometimes I wonder why they can't love me the same way they love my brother. After all, he only brings them trouble. I am the one who looks after them.

It is misleading to assume that any form of oppression affects a group equally and that a subsequent 'liberation from oppression' will be equally enjoyed by all members of that group. Therefore, an in-depth analysis of social and power relations within a group of people is essential in determining the focus of development initiatives and social policy interventions. In addition, we need to remember that there are always exceptions to the rule; in our research, some disabled women were able to do and achieve more than they might have done due to individual factors which worked in their favour — for example particular affection between father and daughter, or family wealth to pay for health-care and education.

When projects targeting disabled people are planned, it is important to take into consideration the fact that women and men will not benefit or be affected equally. This has been demonstrated by the difference in numbers of project beneficiaries when disaggregated by sex. In addition, disabled men seem to be more present in public life than disabled women. Disabled women have needed the extra impetus of family wealth and position to be able to 'succeed in life'. It was evident to us in the course of our research that discrimination starts at home, in the early years of the life of a disabled woman. This discrimination brings with it a reluctance on the part of families, or rather decision makers within the families, to make tangible and intangible resources available to disabled women, thus further undermining their life chances.

It is also essential to understand the way in which associations of disabled persons have dealt with gender issues, and the degree of commitment behind any approach adopted. The creation of special committees and special projects for women need to be questioned, beyond their face value. It is also essential to explore the hidden pressure exerted by funding agencies and the extent to which is this conducive to integrating a gender analysis. A Yemeni woman member of an association of disabled persons told us:

I think it's great that we [women] are now present within the association. But to tell you the truth, they have allowed us to be in only because the funders have insisted on this.

The Friends of the Hanicapped Association provide training and job placement opportunities for women with disabilities in North Lebanon.

The Beijing Conference and follow-up

The UN Fourth Conference on Women was an important event with great potential for impact on the lives of women throughout the world. Globally, preparations leading up to Beijing included extensive research, advocacy, lobbying, networking, and mobilisation of women at country, regional, and international levels. In the case of the Middle East, the lead-up to Beijing, the conference itself, and its aftermath, created an atmosphere conducive to raising gender issues with organisations who had hitherto ignored them. The Beijing conference involved several grassroots NGO organisations who do not perceive themselves as having a clear feminist agenda; these organisations took part alongside women's organisationsr, particularly in the preparatory process.

Almost two years after Beijing, official government follow-up committees and (in most countries) parallel NGO committees have formed, for the task of seeing through the implementation of the Platform of Action agreed in Beijing, and its translation into national Plans of Action. The Beijing Conference has obliged both governments and NGOs to become more accountable to their constituencies, and to the wider international community. Activists in all spheres and at all levels are looking to governments and international bodies to take concrete steps to bring about advancement in the situation and social position of women.

The implementation of National Plans of Action is dependent on substantial resources from various sources, notably governments and UN bodies. Already, country and regional-based planning workshops are being organised to put pressure on these bodies into making resources available, and to determine how resources should be used. Yet, in my experience, it is rare at these planning events to demonstrate awareness and analysis of the specific needs and situation of women with disabilities, and a commitment to addressing them. Failure to consider the particular interests of women with disabilities at this early planning stage will inevitably result in women with disabilities being left out of the Beijing follow-up process, and from the subsequent allocation of the vital resources needed to bring about positive change.

Continuing gender-blindness at disability events

On another level, we also notice a failure to integrate and address gender issues at the planning stage in disability-focused development conferences and events. One example among many is that of the International Labour Organisation (ILO) workshop, held in Yemen in September 1996, to discuss the employment situation of disabled persons and formulate policies and initiatives at the UN and government levels, which omitted to address women's exclusion from the market and how initiatives intended to benefit all disabled people will actually fail to integrate women and men with disabilities equally in the employment market.

Here, the issue is the mirror image of the Beijing follow-up process, which omits the consideration of disability as an issue. Gender-blind planning and policy-making in this sector will reinforce the disadvantaged position of women with disabilities. I would like to recount a recent interview I had with a Canadian lawyer who was conducting a study on the reform of labour laws in Lebanon. The recommendations of the study were to be geared towards particularly vulnerable groups, notably 'the disabled'. A stated aim was to bring about amendments on the labour code to ensure a better integration of 'the disabled' into the workplace, in both public and private sectors. I put it to the lawyer that this policy would not benefit women and men equally, unless specific issues concerning gender were considered. To reinforce my point, I told him about recent appointments within the public sector, which have predominantly benefited disabled men, as disabled women are less able to secure the jobs available. The response was 'well, perhaps if you look at it this way...'. He seemed not ready to consider alternative points of view, even if evidence was provided to support these!

Overall, it is reasonable to assume that, at a time when policy decisions are being taken on allocation of resources, women with disabilities have to struggle to be heard. Perhaps the first problem to be overcome is that of representation, as women with disabilities need to be represented within women's groups and within disability groups. However, at another level, that of funding agencies such as Oxfam UK/I, another process needs to take place: an acknowledgement of the struggle and efforts of women with disabilities to determine their own lives, and a commitment to ensure that policies on resource allocation and capacity-building specifically serve to advance the cause, situation, and position of women with disabilities.

References

Awdeh, M and alHajj, A A (1992) *Focus on the Lives of Disabled Women in Palestinian Society*, Birzeit University (published in Arabic).
Boylan E (1991) *Women And Disability*, Zed Books,London.
Daoud, Z (1993) Politique et Feminisme au Maghreb.
Kabeer, N (1994) *Reversed Realities: Gender Hierarchies in Development Thought*, Verso, London.
Sen, A K 'Gender and co-operation conflicts'in Tinker I *Persistent Inequalities*, OUP, 1990.

3

The case studies

Introduction

This chapter will explore various programme initiatives and the different paths these took to integrate gender in their analysis and ensuing action for change. Whilst these experiences, written by disability activists, NGO workers, and Oxfam staff, are anchored within the context of Lebanon, Yemen, and the Palestinian Territories, the issues they raise will most probably find resonance in other parts of the world.

Sylvana Lakkis, now the president of the Lebanese Sitting Handicapped Association, discusses the creation and development of her association as a movement of people with disabilities. Lakkis argues that discovering how and why disability affects women and men differently was a long process which at various times in its history caused a rift between members of the association. The strategies described for putting gender on the agenda of the association reflect the long-term vision and commitment of the association for ensuring equal rights for both women and men with disabilities.

Houda Boukhari, the director of a centre for children with learning disabilities in Southern Lebanon, highlights the predicament of girls with learning difficulties and of women carers. The article stresses the invisibility of these two categories of girls and women and their subsequent vulnerability to abuse and violence. Boukhari argues that a sound development programme is one that identifies and addresses the vulnerabilities of these women.

The collective article written by the steering committee members of the Youth Association for the Blind in Lebanon refers to the specific experience of exclusion and disadvantage of women with visual impairments. The findings drawn from an in-depth study of blind women in South Lebanon, a disadvantaged area particularly affected by conflict and violence, point out marked differences in making resources available for disabled women in contrast to disabled men, particularly within the same household. This, the authors believe, is the main cause for disadvantaging and undermining the future life-chances of women with visual disabilities and thus furthering their dependence and isolation. The authors move from this to stress the importance of launching programmes and initiatives which specifically target the needs and situation of blind women.

Leila Atshan, a Palestinian blind woman working as a university teacher and psychologist, looks at the different attitudes of society towards women and men with disabilities. Whereas men with disabilities have the privilege of being upheld as heroes in a situation of conflict, women cannot aspire to such privileges. Atshan notes, however, gradual positive attitudinal changes which are currently taking place in addition to exploring further the issue of double-discrimination on the basis of gender and disability.

Suad Ramadan, currently working as a Programme Officer for Oxfam (UKI) in Yemen recounts her experience in working with a local association for people with disability in Yemen. Ramadan critically analyses the impact of Oxfam (UKI), as a foreign funding agency, in furthering gender in the programme of the association and in increasing the representation of women at the decision-making level of the association. The author cautions against a possible backlash when the process is not owned and led by the association in question and invites a more in-depth assessment of the situation and a further stress on capacity building and organisational development.

Finally, in her analysis of the Fourth UN Conference on Women (September 1995), Jahda Abu-Khalil, the director of the National Association for the Rights of Disabled Persons in Lebanon, points out the poor organisation of women with disabilities in the Middle East and Maghreb. Abu-Khalil argues that this has led to the lack of a strong agenda for action, thus minimising the possible gains and positive outcomes from this international event. Abu-Khalil believes that unless serious commitment is placed on mobilisation and organisation, women with disability will be further disadvantaged and their needs given less priority by both the disability and women's movements.

3.1

Mobilising women with physical disabilities: The Lebanese Sitting Handicapped Association

Sylvana Lakkis

Disabled men and women in Lebanon, as in many other parts of the world, were historically neglected, made to feel shame, and faced with many forms of discrimination. People with disabilities were hidden either within their family homes, or within charitable and rehabilitation institutions. Disabled people had to live in a social environment where they were totally ignored, which effectively increased the impact of their disability.

Although blind people were the first to organise in Lebanon (in the mid-1960s), they did not try to create pressure groups to demand change to the living conditions of disabled persons. An impetus towards this came first from people with physical disabilities, who began to organise in 1981, rebelling against the outrageous conditions they experienced within rehabilitation institutions. They came from different parts of the country, and belonged to different religious denominations. The creation of this organisation of disabled people, the Lebanese Sitting Handicapped Association (LSHA), coincided with the declaration of the UN International Decade of the Disabled (1981–1990).

In the years before the founding of LSHA, and since, we have campaigned in all parts of Lebanon, calling for individual disabled people to join our association. We believe that disabled people should represent themselves and should join forces in order to become a 'critical mass' able to exert pressure on the government and on civil society. Our work and campaigns stress the need for equal opportunities, and unrestricted access to services, for disabled people, and the need to raise public awareness about the issue of disability. We were able to extend and set up branches of our association in almost all the provinces in the country, drawing in hundreds of members and volunteers. In addition to our grassroots mobilisation work, we developed an advocacy programme and co-operated with other associations of disabled persons formed later in the 1980s. Getting support for our advocacy work was difficult. Whereas international agencies were willing to fund services and projects run by a large association, very few had faith in what we were trying to do.

It soon became obvious to us that disability as such cannot be treated separately from other socio-economic issues. Not only does this further marginalise and isolate people with disabilities, and their cause, but it also obscures the important relations which exist between socio-economic and political issues and the public attitude towards disability. We realised that, as disabled people, we needed to address the problems of poverty and we also needed to have a presence and a say in all public issues and debates. Ours should not be seen as a cause apart, but as an element of more general developmental, economic, and social issues. We also realised that we needed to be more professional in our work, and move on from our initial way of working where we were emotionally driven, and aiming solely at drawing solidarity from the non-disabled community.

Disabled people need to have a presence and a say in all public issues and debates. Disabled people taking part in a peace march, November 1987

Thinking about gender issues

Originally, our ways of working were inspired by the trade union movement. We felt all disabled people needed to work together, joined by a common struggle. We felt we were all equal in this struggle, and that ultimately, once we win our rights, then we will all reap the benefits of these years of hard work. But slowly, we began to notice that things were far more complicated than we thought. To move on, hard data and facts about the disabled were necessary. There are virtually no statistics in the Lebanon to refer to, so we decided to survey our own constituency. We conducted a survey in the five areas where we have branches: Beirut, Saida, Nabatieh, Byblos, and Baalbek, extending all over the country. We have found that out of the total disabled persons surveyed (1870), 80 per cent are totally illiterate. Out of these, 82 per cent are women. Only 2 per cent have access to some form of services. These are mainly concentrated in Beirut and to some extent in Saida, and reflect the concentration of services for disabled persons in major cities. Of our respondents, 5 per cent have skills in simple handcrafts (20 per cent of whom are women), whereas only 2 per cent describe themselves as totally independent both financially and personally. Of these, very few are women.

Our findings confirmed that the disabled women we work with are far more unfortunate than their male comrades. We also found that the situation of disabled women varied according to geographical location. In those areas where women are in general more secluded, less mobile, and have less access to education and employment, we have found that disabled women share these constraints, but added to this face particular forms of gender discrimination due to their disability.

We have also found that within households where more than one person is disabled — these households are quite common in Lebanon — a disabled son is treated differently from his disabled sister. A striking example is a case of a brother and sister, both with motor disability. While the family managed to secure a wheelchair for the son, no such efforts were deemed necessary for his sister.

I was personally involved in following up the case of a woman, Nadia, who became tetraplegic after a car accident. She was a few months pregnant with her second daughter. As soon as he found out that she was to become disabled for life, her husband repudiated her and remarried another young woman. Nadia had to go through the trauma of her new disability, as well as her pregnancy and delivery by herself, having lost her family and her job. In fact, the religious family code makes it possible for a man to divorce his wife and claim immediate child custody if she becomes chronically sick or disabled.

Even within our association, which saw itself as egalitarian in many ways, an in-depth investigation revealed fewer women than men members, fewer women seeking advice and services, and fewer women on the general assembly and steering committee.

Later on in 1992, I was attending a conference organised by Disabled People International (DPI) in Vancouver, Canada. This is where I met for the first time organisations and committees of disabled women whose agenda was, if not separate from the mainstream disabled groups, focusing on the specific needs and problems of disabled women. Meeting these women was an enlightening experience for me and colleagues in our association. We began to discuss our own personal histories and recollect stories that other women had told us. It was daunting to realise how much worse off we were than disabled men. It was then that we decided to do something about it.

Disabled women coming together

Organisations of disabled persons are mostly led by disabled men, and only occasionally and temporarily do disabled women have any decision-making roles. In fact, although our associations tend to challenge discrimination and prejudice against the disabled, they fail to see and address the similar prejudices which exist against disabled women on grounds of their sex. Until very recently, lobbying and advocacy undertaken by the disabled movement was male-oriented, despite the fact that all groups of disabled persons insist that they themselves do not practise any sex discrimination.

When we looked closely at our own association, we realised that discrimination occurs in various unconscious ways. Many examples can be given to illustrate this. While we welcome any disabled person who comes to us, those seeking membership of our association, or information or services, are for the most part disabled men. When we go about meeting disabled people in their homes and we try to recruit them to become members, we rarely face resistance from families when the disabled person is a man. When the disabled person is a woman, the task requires far more time and effort, and we are not always successful. We have not yet investigated why this is so. Possible reasons for women's not joining our organisation include, first, that the vocational training courses we offer to disabled women are traditional and of questionable value. To start with, we assumed that it would be appropriate for disabled women to learn knitting and sewing and for disabled men to learn electrical installation and computing. We noticed that while our organisation was able to claim a number of achievements in terms of job placements, vocational training, and mainstreaming of disabled people in the regular education system, the beneficiaries were mostly disabled men. Whereas it was possible to see disabled men in public life who have attained respected positions, it was virtually impossible for disabled women to do so even if they came from well-to-do families.

Those lucky disabled women who were able to find jobs often reported discrimination in pay, and physical and sexual harassment at work and while using public transport. When the Ministry of Energy approved a recommendation put forward by the disability lobby to hire qualified disabled persons, 54 were recruited. This was an unprecedented case of positive action on disability. However, only four of these 54 were women. We also lobbied for recruitment of disabled people in a factory manufacturing electrical appliances. Eighteen disabled were hired, all of whom were men.

Discrimination is also evident in organisations which state that they are concerned with the rights and well-being of the disabled. While lobbying and challenging the big rehabilitation institutions, it did not at first occur to us to look at the sex discrimination that they practise on a larger scale.

The Lebanese Sitting Handicapped Association, Beirut, is one of the first associations of disabled persons in Lebanon to have formed a women's committee.

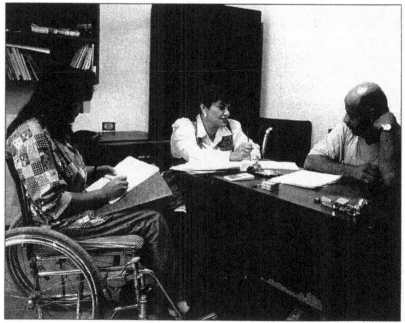

Chris Johnson/Oxfam

With all the above in mind, and with the support of Oxfam, we decided to form a women's committee within our association. We have opted for this strategy because we felt that we wanted to remain within the disability movement rather than outside it. Also, rather than attacking the movement for being unaware of the needs of women, we wanted to promote change from within. Our task was to build awareness, and ensure that no form of direct or indirect discrimination is practised towards disabled women within our association. It was important to provide our own colleagues with convincing data about how disabled women are disadvantaged, and concrete examples of what we should be doing about this. Our longer-term goals were to develop a programme which directly addresses gender issues related to disabled women, and to place gender issues centrally in our advocacy work.

We proceeded in small and hesitant steps. We focused first on getting to know our physically disabled women members better. We also wanted to know what they felt about LSHA. Did they think it represents them, in which ways had it made their life better, and what should be done to ensure that LSHA represents their needs and concerns better? We agreed with LSHA's steering committee that we should review, from a gender perspective, each of the activities and projects with which LSHA was involved. We felt we needed to be the voice who keeps asking: 'what about women?'

From sport to computing: challenging stereotypes

From that, we moved into the more concrete activity of proposing and implementing new initiatives for women. This was the most challenging step, as its failure or success would determine our future as the women's committee within LSHA. We proceeded by forming the first disabled women's sports team in Lebanon (in fact, this is only the second in the Middle East region). We chose sports purposely because of all the taboos attached to the active participation of women, notably disabled women, in sports. We believed that an all-disabled women's team would, amongst other things, increase the visibility of disabled women and encourage others to come out of their isolation. The team attracted many young women, prompting them to challenge taboos in their families and communities. After months of arduous training, the team participated successfully in a number of local and regional competitions. However, perhaps its main achievement was the high morale of its members, and the fame it gained within LSHA!

More recently, we have turned our attention to challenging the stereotypes surrounding 'appropriate' employment for women; we have organised computer training courses for more than 50 disabled women and men. Following this activity, we successfully lobbied for the recruitment of 27 women and 28 men trainees with the Ministry of Communications.

Programme planning changes

We have been able to introduce a new mandatory requirement in our programme planning process. Branches and project leaders are now expected to demonstrate how their work is intended to benefit disabled women, and how it actually affects them. This is a very difficult task for everybody, and in particular for the women's committee itself. Having gone this far, we discovered that we need much more knowledge, and additional skills. The next step in our strategy is to develop the skills of the committee.

I attended the Fourth UN Conference on Women in Beijing, in September 1995, as a representative of LSHA. Beijing was a very important event for us. It stirred heated debates within LSHA and the women's committee, which resulted in an official commitment from LSHA to adopt genderissues as part of its remit and mandate.

Towards a wider representation of disabled women

Disabled women in Lebanon have been so far almost totally absent from the public arena and at both the public and NGO levels. They are ignored by development NGOs and by women's groups, and are not seen as a priority by disabled groups. We need to infiltrate all these strongholds. If the disability movement persists in ignoring the situation of disabled women, then it does not represent all people with disabilities. On the other hand, if women's groups do not have the issue of disability clearly on their agenda, then their movement also fails to represent all women.

Over the past few years, I feel that our best reward was in finding other disabled and able-bodied sisters in LSHA and beyond, who understand how and why disabled women are treated differently, and who have decided to do something about this. We still have quite a long way to go, and many obstacles to overcome. There are still many sceptical voices, who do not see the point of 'favouring disabled women', as they put it. We are fully aware that any change in the situation of women with disabilities can only come about when there is a real change in the general situation of women in our country and region. At the time of writing, progress is greatly threatened by a rapid regression to political conservatism in many parts of our region. The worsening economic situation is also threatening disabled women's already meagre chances of obtaining education and employment.

Sylvana Lakkis is currently the president of the Lebanese Sitting Handicapped Association and the founder of LSHA's women's committee. She has participated in the Fourth UN Conference on Women in Beijing in September 1996. She has had polio since her early childhood and lived in Czechoslovakia, where she received treatment and studied to become an interpreter.

3.2

Invisible victims: working with mothers of children with learning disabilities

Houda Boukhari

In 1986, when the Happy Home Centre was founded, our initial intention was to work with families as well as children. Yet it was not obvious to us then — as it is now — that the heart of the problem facing woman carers is not the practical fact of disability itself, but an age-old system which oppresses women, puts them in an inferior position to men in their households, and blames them for anything that goes wrong, including the birth of a disabled child. During the course of our work, we have witnessed different ways in which women carers and their disabled children, boys and girls, are oppressed and abused. In trying to compile some of the most dramatic instances, it became obvious to the team that some of these situations are shared by women in general. It also became obvious how a child's disability increases the workload and suffering of an already ill-treated mother.

In this short article, based on a presentation which I made during the UN IV Conference on Women held in Beijing (September 1995), I will try to describe briefly the experience I and my colleagues have gained through the Happy Home Centre: an experience which has led us to identify women carers as a central focus for our work with disabled children. I describe how we subsequently developed an understanding and broader analysis of issues affecting women as applicable in our specific situation. Our work has evolved to include addressing the issue of how gender inequality affects not only the lives of disabled women and girls, but those women who care for disabled family members.

For reasons of space, this article concentrates in the main on those women carers who live within the child's household, and are responsible for caring for the child in a family context. I hope that this article may prove helpful in assisting others to develop useful strategies, in the Middle East and beyond, for work with women carers.

The context

In the Lebanese context, the birth of a disabled child is seen by many as not only a misfortune, but as shameful and embarrassing. The husband's family is likely to blame the misfortune on the mother: 'it is her [family's] bad seed...' In addition to bringing shame on the family, the birth of a disabled child is likely to consign his or her mother to a lifetime of misery, since the belief in the mother's culpability is used to justify a lack of practical and emotional support to the child and mother on the part of the husband and extended family. After all, isn't it the mother's fault in the first place? Many of the women we know are deeply convinced that they should feel this guilt, and that they should atone for it until the end of their lives. If the mother dies, one of the daughters must take over the burden of shame and responsibility.

In Lebanon, as in other countries around the world, attitudes to institutionalising children and adults with disabilities have changed over time. While families historically cared for children with learning disabilities (often referred to as mental disabilities), during this century there has been a trend to confining such children in special institutions. It is only relatively recently that this practice has been questioned. One function of such institutions was to rid families of the daily care of children who were stigmatised by being seen as 'abnormal'; institution-alisation meant that they could be kept away from their families and communities.

In Lebanon, the last decade has witnessed the emergence of parents' groups and small associations, which provide special education and rehabilitation for children with learning disabilities, while they live at home with their families. The Happy Home Centre, founded in 1986, is one of these. The idea which led to the opening of the centre was to provide individual care and education to children with learning disabil-ities, to work with their families and raise awareness of social issues relating to disability. With its stress on supporting the right of disabled children to become independent and integrated into community life, and its work with the mothers of these children, the Happy Home Centre is adopting a new approach to education for children with disabilities. Its day-care services do not need to be advertised: people find out about the Centre by personal recommendation. There is a nominal monthly charge to cover transport and sundry expenses, equivalent to about £12 per month.

The work of the Happy Home Centre

At the beginning of the Happy Home Centre's existence, our work was divided into three main areas: a Special Education Programme implemented within the centre, a Family Outreach Programme, and a Social Awareness and Consciousness-Raising Programme, aiming to alter the social environment in which the children live.

At the outset, we spent time getting to know the children: their needs, aptitudes, specific problems, likes and dislikes. This helped us to decide what to do with them, but also made us realise the tremendous challenges and difficulties lying ahead. We also needed to get to know their families; a major component of our work is home-visiting. Working with disabled children necessarily entails close co-operation with families, and an understanding on their part of the special needs of their children, and the significance of our work with them.

This part of our work was an eye-opener into the complex problems faced by household members. The average family size is seven (actually ranging from five to fourteen among families with whom we work). This is large in terms of providing for the cost of basic education and health services. Disabled children not only require constant attention, and can often be a source of nuisance, but in addition, their care requires a significant share of the family's already over-stretched financial resources.

Most if not all of the children we are involved with come from very poor families, and live in dire socio-economic conditions. Almost half of the families are refugees, living in the Palestinian refugee camps around Sidon. The majority of the others are families displaced from the south of Lebanon, because of Israeli military attacks. Of the 60 fathers of children with whom we were working during the 1994-95 school year, 43 were illiterate or had minimal elementary education.

Economic activity is rare, save for small individual businesses. The overwhelming majority of parents, mostly fathers, who are daily labourers, are not protected by any labour law or social security system. They have no job security and no social and health services or pension scheme to fall back on. Most of them are daily construction or agricultural labourers, or have low-paid clerical jobs. Of the 60 mothers, 49 are illiterate, or have received minimal elementary education; only five of them worked, as house cleaners, street vendors, and agricultural labourers.

Whether in refugee camps or outside them, families live in small and overcrowded houses with appalling environmental and health conditions, including open sewers running close to damp houses, and no rubbish collection services. In addition, a combination of poverty and the social dislocation caused by war and the presence of armed forces make the streets in these areas unsafe, especially for women and children.

Chris Mowles/Oxfam

The Happy Home Centre not only provides educational facilities for children with learning disabilities, but also supports mothers of disabled children.

Being a poor mother of a disabled child

Although poverty affects both women and men, women are much more sharply hit in the sense that when resources are scarce, it is likely that men and boys will get whatever little is available. For example, families are quick to take their daughters out of school during difficult times, as not only does this save on the cost of tuition fees, but girls at home can provides domestic help for their overworked mothers. (I should emphasise that this does not imply that their brothers all complete their schooling, as some of the brothers may also be forced to drop out of school to start work early and help to sustain the family.) Thus, girls learn only to become housewives: a future where education and independence have no place. Among the families with whom we work, it is mostly, if not uniquely, daughters who share with their mothers the responsibility of caring for a disabled brother or sister. Some help may come from grandmothers, depending on whether the grandmother is related to the mother (when she will probably give help and support) or father (when she is less likely to help).

The fate of able-bodied daughters who do not attend school is effectively pre-determined, and there is very little that they, or their mothers, can say or do to challenge this. Needless to say, while there are few resources to be invested for able-bodied girls, there are not likely to be any at all for disabled girls. Mothers typically have little say in decisions about the future of their children: Randa, aged eight, was making wonderful progress with us, but was recently taken out of the centre by her mother. Her mother wanted her to continue attending, and was extremely upset. However, she was compelled to remove Randa from the centre by her husband and sons, who deemed it morally unacceptable that their daughter and sister be taught dancing at school. They felt that Randa had better stay at home and help with the housework.

In addition to undermining their chances of finding paid work, illiteracy further exacerbates the dependence and lower status of women within their families. In addition to the general socio-economic pressure shared by all family members, women carers suffer from additional social, traditional, and health pressure. For example, restriction on mobility is another factor binding these women to their homes, their households, and their reproductive role.

Many women we have talked to report that they suffer from health problems, many of which are related to their reproductive health. Multiparity is a frequent, if not a common and accepted fact of life. Women have no control over their bodies, and cultural norms oblige them to bear many children in quick succession. The rationale for this is, in part, concerned with male gender ideology: many children are a visible proof of the man's virility. It is also economic: a large family is likely to contain many sons, who can earn an income and increase family wealth.

As a result of multiple pregnancies, often in poor hygienic conditions, the women we work with typically suffer from a number of health problems. Many have continued to give birth after the age of 45 or even 50, thus increasing the likelihood of bearing children with disabilities. In fact, almost half of the children attending our centre were born to multiparous mothers who were over 45 years of age. Not only does age affect the mother's chances of giving birth to a disabled child, but also makes her less able to cope with the arduous work which caring for some of these children entails. These mothers, who may already have a large family to care for, are often physically and psychologically exhausted by the numerous births, and by caring, often alone, for all their children.

If an individual woman questions the principle that she should give birth to a large family, or attempts to rebel against this, the threat of repudiation (a particular form of divorce whereby the man has the right to expel his wife from their home), or that her husband will marry a second wife, is always lurking in the background.

Violence and abuse of disabled children

In many cases, this state of affairs is further exacerbated by chronic domestic violence by men, mainly against their wives but also against their children, both able-bodied and disabled. In a context where for many women, physical and other forms of violence and abuse are all too common, the presence of the disabled child is seen as an additional excuse for violence by the man, and in many cases this becomes the only form of communication. For example, Fadia, a 12-year-old who has attended our centre for five years now, has often shown unusual behaviour especially after long stays with her family (week-ends and school holidays). She was often sore and itchy and had bruises on her face and body. We were aware of the physical violence of her father towards her and her mother and were attempting to co-operate with other NGOs in trying to address this issue. However, our concern increased when Fadia told one of the trainers that her father insists that she sleeps naked next to him every night. This polygamous man was also in the habit of watching pornographic films in front of his children (unavoidable, since all the family lived in one room). He also shared the same bed with his two co-wives and his daughters.

Violence and abuse also come from outside the family. Again, disabled girls are a target. The team discovered three cases of disabled girls attending the centre being raped by men in the area where they live. The rapists were members of armed militias, and the families were scared to press charges. Not only would this carry the risk of reprisal from the offenders but would also bring more shame to the family which is already stigmatised for having a disabled daughter.

Helping women carers: a strategy for action

Perhaps the first step in helping women carers is to recognise, and try to understand, the problems and the issues. We have come to realise that working with children alone is of limited efficacy: our work needs to extend to include the family. However, as outlined above, targeting the family inevitably reveals fundamental problems within the household: taboos and tradition, the superior position of the male head of the household, and of course, overarching all, is the vicious cycle of poverty.

Education

We consider education to be a main tool for empowering the women with whom we work. Though we cannot provide literacy courses, we seek to mitigate the negative impact of illiteracy, and when possible with the co-operation of other NGOs, encourage women to join classes for adults. Considerable time is spent with mothers in exchanging information about the child, explaining the purpose of the educational programme he or she follows at the Happy Home Centre, and trying to reach agreement over the role that parents, and particularly mothers, need to play. It is through such discussions, on an individual, personal basis, that we first begin to understand the different problems which beset the households with whom we are involved.

Through group seminars and individual discussions around health and preventive health care, we are able to tackle taboos and sensitive issues, such as reproductive health, including family planning and sexual education. Group activities are held with other NGOs working in the area. This allows women to develop new contacts, and engage in activities outside their homes.

Following on from these general activities, smaller and more systematic discussion groups for mothers were formed. These have provided a haven for women, enabling them to forget their responsibilities for a short time, and giving each woman the opportunity to talk about personal aspects of her life. These sessions have created a sense of solidarity amongst mothers.

Parents' committee

A parents' committee has been formed; one of its aims was to encourage women to take on leadership and decision-making roles. (It should be noted that most of the members of the parents' committee are mothers. Fathers are often unable to find the time to attend since they are attempting to earn income; for some fathers, too, issues related to their disabled children are of little interest.) Women in this committee have shown a high degree of active participation, enthusiasm and commitment. The committee has also allowed many of them to discover and develop new skills, and engage in activities which are beyond the usual household chores.

Promoting fathers' participation

Because the women we work with are overburdened, we have gradually started working with them on time-management training. Although we are well aware that this does not address the root of their problem of over-work, we feel that a better control of their time may eventually allow them to claim some time for themselves. In addition to encouraging fathers to understand the need of mothers to have a little time to themselves, we also promote the participation of fathers in the care of their disabled children. So far, we have had limited success; we have been most successful with fathers who are members of the parents' committee, whom, we assume, are already better aware of the need to share with their wives the care of their disabled child. We have not been able to work in this way with any of the abusive fathers.

Eradicating violence

So far, we have been least successful in addressing the issue of family violence. Faced with such a grave and disconcerting problem, we are currently feeling that we lack the skills to undertake any valuable intervention. There are no organisations in Lebanon (whether governmental or non-governmental) that we know of who provide any form of assistance to women victims of violence. We have, however, been successful to some extent in tackling the issue of domestic violence against disabled girls and their siblings. This has been possible because the strategy used was a mixture of friendly advice to fathers, and the threat of barring the child from the centre: an effective threat, though one which has never yet been carried out. Fathers are the main perpetrators of such violence, with brothers coming next.

Unfortunately, however, the issue of sexual aggression against able-bodied and disabled women by strangers remains largely unaddressed, owing to the fact that aggressors are mostly armed military men, who have been above the law until now. It is unlikely that any breakthrough will be achieved in this area without close co-operation with other NGOs, the legal system, and those in charge of law-enforcement.

Caring for our carers

We realised that if we were to address 'women's issues' seriously, we could not have double standards when it comes to our own staff. We felt that the association should provide an example, for parents and for the community. We are aware of the immense pressures that female professional carers face, both at work and within their households.

It is no coincidence that the overwhelming majority of professional carers for the disabled are women. These jobs are not normally seen as professional or rewarding careers. They are viewed as suitable for women as they involve an extension of the domestic roles of nursing and nurturing. Professional or academic training relating to this kind of work is almost non-existent, making these jobs even less prestigious. Such jobs are often poorly paid, and time and effort-consuming. Many women end up completely burnt-out, after working for only a few years. For many women, therefore, the jobs are thought of as a temporary 'stop-gap' — a stepping stone to a better-paid job, or marriage.

It is, therefore, important to give attention to improving the situation of women staff in the centre. We have invested time and effort in valuing the job itself and the contribution of each of the staff members. Each was encouraged to discover her own interests and strengths, and was given the opportunity to develop these through training, and taking a lead in a particular aspect of the programme. We have also lobbied our association successfully for better working conditions for women, particularly improved maternity leave and benefits. What we are doing with women carers is but a drop in the ocean, but for the team, it has become an essential part of working with disabled children.

Staff training, although an essential and necessary ingredient for success, should not revolve principally around special education. Training should empower professional carers, mostly women, to allow them to tackle root problems of gender inequality in their own private lives and enable them to understand how disability acts to further undermine and oppress women. Most importantly, training and programme planning should take into consideration the fact that professional women carers may well be suffering from similar conditions as the women with whom they are dealing.

Conclusion

In the long term, for such efforts as ours to succeed in having a real impact on the lives of women carers and their children, more significant changes need to occur in the lives of women. These mostly entail a change in the laws and customs which place women in an inferior position compared to men, and which grant them fewer rights and privileges as mothers and workers.

We have found it to be virtually futile to focus our work solely around the condition, or disability, of the child. Doing so has proved to have little, if any, impact. It is essential to understand the complex relations that exist between poverty, disability, and gender inequality. Furthermore, we are often inclined to forget about the women carers because they are non-disabled.

Finally, I wish to stress that the intention of this paper is not to generalise about the situation of women carers and disabled children in Lebanon in a simplistic way. Our hope is that, based on a compilation of observations and hands on experience over the past nine years, we have been able to convey our sense of the intricate relationship which exists between gender inequality and disability in our context.

Houda Boukhari has a degree in sociology from the Lebanese University. She has worked as a special educator in the Happy Home since 1986 and has been the centre's director since 1990. Besides her work at the Happy Home, she is very much involved in NGO work in Suite, particularly women-related issues. She participated in the Fourth UN Conference on Women (Beijing, September 1995) where she was closely involved in discussions on girls and women with disabilities.

A double discrimination: blind girls' life-chances

Nada Fahd, Maha Marji, Nirmin Mufti,
Muzna Masri and Amer Makaram

My brother and I were both born blind. My father sent only my brother to school in Beirut. I shall never forgive him for this.
Radia, a 29-year-old woman from Nabatieh, born blind

The Youth Association for the Blind is a relatively new association in Lebanon, set up in 1989 by young visually-impaired women and men. Although blind people were the first group of disabled people to organise in Lebanon and in the Arab world at large, the pioneer associations were not involved in lobbying and advocacy on disabled rights. In contrast, our association was driven by young people with a degree of social and political awareness and a concern for rights and equality.

The steering committee, which includes blind and sighted men and women, decided to undertake what was considered by many as a some-what futile activity: to investigate the work of the association, and the extent to which this takes account of gender-related differences. The first indicator sought was quantitative: the number of women at different levels in the organisation, and those who were beneficiaries of our projects and programmes. We found that at the administrative and management level, the percentage of women varied between 12 and 50 per cent, while among project beneficiaries, the proportion of women and girls varied between 30 and 55 per cent. It was only when we looked at subscribers to our university books recording service that we found a high percentage of women involved: 80 per cent. We postulated that the reason why we were attracting fewer women was not only because of their disability, but because of the mere fact of their being women. If this assumption is correct, then if our work is truly aimed at improving the well-being of blind people, we need to understand better the different situations in which blind women and blind men live.

With this in mind, a small study of six blind women from South Lebanon was planned. Our aim was to gain an objective and in-depth understanding of the life experiences of these women, in order to appreciate the nature of the discrimination that they had to deal with and which constrained their lives. We felt that only if we understood the complexities of events taking place at home and within the immediate surrounding environment, would we be able to shape our intervention to address the specific problems of blind women effectively. We have tried in this short paper to explain why we embarked on the research, and to summarise the main findings; finally, we have identified particular points of direct relevance to our work.

The history of our association

The association started its work in Beirut, where we were able to attract a number of young volunteers from both sexes. Our work started with adults, with whom we were trying to develop strategies to overcome or mitigate the effects of a disabling environment. There was a dearth of educational books, at both school and university levels, in taped or braille versions accessible to blind and visually impaired students. Thus, for those blind people who were able to enter mainstream education, success was jeopardised by the unavailability of books. We set up the first public 'talking library' in the country. Initially, we recorded school and university books upon request and also produced a four-monthly taped magazine.

Gradually, after working with adults for a time, we realised that there were fundamental problems in the education of blind and visually-impaired people, which started in childhood. The segregation of blind children in special schools not only serves to increase their isolation, but also creates an artificial, sheltered environment. This makes it extremely difficult for them to cope with the outside world when they leave the institution.

We therefore lobbied for the full integration of blind children in mainstream education, from the early years of childhood. We believed that, given adequate and careful investment in the educational system, as well as close follow-up and monitoring of children and their families, blind children have a good chance of performing well in schools. We started a pilot programme to integrate blind children in mainstream primary school education. With the geographical expansion of our association, this programme also expanded to include boys and girls from different parts of the country.

It was through this programme that we saw the first indications of the huge differences which exist between the position of blind girls and blind boys. Not only was there a relatively low percentage of girls involved in our programme (girls now constitute 40 per cent of the total beneficiaries); in addition, our social workers faced major difficulties when working with the parents of blind girls. Parents were extremely wary of sending their blind girls to school, whereas they were far more compliant when the child was a boy.

In our periodical reviews of the project, it became clear that we were more successful with boys than with girls. Despite the fact that this pilot project earned us a reputation in implementing theories of integration, we were dissatisfied at the limited achievements and problems faced when working with blind girls. However, very few other associations seemed even to notice the obvious inequalities related to gender.

Souraya's story

Perhaps the most striking event for us in our journey towards awareness of the ways in which gender inequality profoundly affects the chances and experiences of disabled women was the marriage of one of our colleagues, a blind woman and a founding member of YAB. Souraya was a most competent, dedicated, and courageous woman. She worked as a telephone operator in a financial institution, a job she was over-qualified for given her university degree, but which enabled her to be financially independent.

Souraya married an unemployed young man who came to live in her house and showed no intention of wanting to work. After marriage, he forced her to wear the veil, and insisted she gave up her responsibilities in the association, since this was not bringing them any financial benefit. However, he did not mind her staying in her paid job and taking care of the household. The concessions that Souraya had to make came as something of a shock to us. She was one of the rare blind women who ever married, let alone married an able-bodied man. The price she had to pay in return was exorbitant. Souraya's experience became particularly significant for us when we compared it with that of the relatively high number of blind men who marry sighted women. The fate of these wives is to become unremunerated and unrecognised carers for their husbands.

Research methodology

We chose to locate our study in the southern province of Nabatieh, where YAB is the only operating organisation of blind people. Nabatieh, officially considered as a 'remote rural area', has a large majority of Muslim

Shi'ites in its population, and a small Christian community. The nearest schools for the blind are in Beirut. Six blind and visually impaired women, aged between 16 and 36, were selected. All had an involvement with the association in one form or another, which prompted us to investigate the perceived role that YAB had played in their lives. We think that our well-established relationship with each of the women positively affected their responses, which appeared extremely open and straightforward.

Our main research method was to collect oral histories from our inter-viewees. The interview form we used consisted of open-ended questions dealing with the perceived role of parents, making a distinction between the roles of mothers and fathers; and the discrimination experienced as between blind men and blind women, and between blind women and sighted women, in respect of education, work, and social networks.

Most of the women interviewed were functionally illiterate, having had only two to three years of primary education before being with-drawn from school, either because of poor achievement or arbitrary family decision. They all came from very impoverished farming families. Most had totally illiterate mothers, whereas their fathers tended to have received slightly more education.

Main findings

In our environment, family life is ruled by traditions and strict religious guidance, which give fathers absolute authority over their families. Mothers cater for the day-to-day maintenance of their households, including caring for children. They do not have the social or religious authority to make any significant decisions regarding their children. For example, decisions about the mobility of girls are always taken by fathers.

Education

Our research confirmed that it is fathers who decide whether or not girls should go to school. The father of one of our respondents, Randa, was against sending girls, sighted or blind, to schools. 'Why should girls learn to read and write?' she reported him saying: 'so that they can write letters to their lovers?' Randa told us that she thinks this is probably why her three older sisters were never allowed to go to school, unlike her brothers. (Although fathers decide whether or not their children should go to school, the decision about completing his education is left to the male child, who is considered mature enough to take on such responsibility.)

The fact that schooling, albeit modest in quality, is available near at hand means that in theory it would be possible for sighted girls to receive some degree of education. The situation of blind girls is very different, because the only schools for the blind are in Beirut. None of the six respondents were allowed by their fathers to attend these special schools. This is not surprising, given that these institutions are all co-educational boarding schools.

The most important form of discrimination is between blind women and blind men. In one striking example, a blind woman was not allowed to go to a school for the blind whereas her blind brother was. This has inevitable repercussions on the future prospects of blind men and women. With opportunities for employment for the blind already scarce, uneducated blind women find themselves lacking any marketable skills. This explains why none of our respondents are gainfully employed.

Employment

We noticed many similarities between blind girls and their sighted sisters in terms of employment. While no girls were engaged in gainful employment outside their homes, their brothers who had left school had freely chosen their occupations and means of livelihood. It is our view that the lack of education and training which would make them employable is a result of restrictions imposed on blind women as a result of their gender, rather than their disabilities.

Social life and marriage

Similar observations were made with respect to involvement in social life and social networks. Since girls, whether blind or sighted, are not allowed to leave home to go to school or to work, they are also not allowed to have their own social life outside their home and immediate family. All blind women interviewed asserted that this rule was enforced particularly strictly when it came to having any form of relationship with men. Restrictions on blind women leaving their homes are particularly severe, both because they are seen as bringing shame on the family because of their disability, and also because they are less capable of defending themselves against abuse. (The latter fear is well-founded: there are many reported cases of blind women being assaulted in institutions, work-places, and on public transport.) At least three of the respondents reported not having left the house for years until YAB got in touch with them. However, when it came to roles and responsibilities within the household, blind girls and their sighted sisters were equally expected to participate in household chores.

Gender discrimination at the level of marriage, the only acceptable form of relationship between the two sexes, is even more marked. Most of our respondents dismissed the possibility of marriage, because of their blindness. Dunia, who had become blind as an adult, reported that she had had a love affair when she was still able-bodied. When she became blind, her lover left her. 'This is normal' she says, 'there is no way that a sighted man will accept a blind woman as his lifetime partner.' Most respondents, however, felt that it is both possible and 'normal' for blind men to marry sighted women, which is consistent with our earlier observations.

The results of the study

This small study allowed us to observe more similarities between blind women and sighted women than between blind women and blind men. It is therefore quite wrong to assume that blind women and blind men will benefit equally from our work. For all the women interviewed, their contact to date with YAB has provided an outlet and a window to the outside world. They reported that it has taken considerable effort for their parents to be convinced of the need to provide an opportunity for their blind daughters to get out of the house and interact with other people.

Aspirations for the future

Our respondents had very different aspirations for the future, and we were unable to discern reasons behind these variations. Some wished to return to school, to study, to obtain a degree; others to learn a skill and become self-employed; others simply wished to find employment of some sort. The common factor observed was that all wanted to become 'financially independent and help their families'; to be productive members of their families. None reported the aspiration of marrying and having children, which would be the normal response expected from young women in this society.

Conclusion

Whilst it was crucial to begin by looking at the ways in which sex discrimination begins at home, we now need to become more knowledgeable about the ways in which sex discrimination manifests itself in our communities, and how it is further exacerbated by disability, to the point that any family investment in a blind woman appears to be pointless. Our strategy for the future needs to be broader; we must research how discrimination within the community and at the policy-making level affects disabled women. As a result of our research, we have come to the conclusion that unless we develop specific strategies to target blind women, our work will remain incomplete.

Nada Fahd, Maha Marji, Nirmin Mufti, Muzna Masri, and Amer Makaram are all members of the Youth Association for the Blind.

Disability and gender at a cross-roads: a Palestinian perspective

Leila Atshan

The issues of disability and gender cannot be divorced from their socio-economic and historical context. It is widely recognised nowadays that disability must be studied as part of a cultural matrix, affected by other important factors such as gender, and economic and political status. All these considerations condition any approach taken by Western development practitioners and funders attempting to confront the issue of disability in the Middle East region.

Palestine, as a region in the Middle East, is in some ways an anomaly. The land of Palestine has long been a cultural icon to the West; it is the 'Holy Land' in Christian religion. Palestine is also regarded in the language of development economics as part of the 'Third World'. It is also seen by Arabs as an occupied territory. Palestine and Israel have received a good deal of worldwide media attention recently, because of the process of the peace talks, the declaration of a Palestinian state, the resurgence of violence, and the recent elections bringing the Likud party back to power.

I will start by looking briefly at historical attitudes towards disabled people, held by Palestinians themselves. Traditionally, disability has been synonymous with shame. The presence of a disabled family member was perceived as a blight on the honour and reputation of the entire unit. Consequently, disabled people have been marginalised and shunned socially, to the point of invisibility. For the family, disability can mean guilt by association. Merely being related to a disabled person could damage marriage prospects, due to the fear of impairment continuing down the line, through successive generations. Often, disability, particularly when congenital, is viewed as a sign of divine intervention or the work of evil spirits (*djinn*). Associated with this is the idea that disability is contagious; a logical response to this is to isolate the disabled person.

While male children have an economic significance within the family, female children carry a symbolic value; this is in line with the fact that women are, in many cultures, viewed as symbols of family worth and honour. The health and beauty of girls and women are a representation of family well-being, and a symbol of the good standing of the family. Female family members are not usually expected to produce wealth independently; they are primarily seen as mothers, supporting the lead of fathers, brothers and, ultimately, their husbands. It is expected that all daughters will marry; a successful arranged marriage is an enhancement to the family's name and prestige.

Because of these norms of female beauty and the role of women in the family, a disabled woman is seen as a failure on several counts. While disabled sons can be tolerated and often married, disabled daughters are merely a drain on already stretched resources; permanent family members, with no hope of future marriage or social mobility. It is quite usual for a disabled woman to be kept hidden by her family. This can mean imprisonment in the home, locked in a single room, without any visitors beyond the immediate family. The mode of care for the disabled in charitable institutions in many ways followed this tradition. Disabled people can be housed in establishments further removed from the family and the community; thus the problem is solved, and the individual conveniently, as it were, ceases to exist. It is common for many people living in institutional care to receive no family visitors whatsoever.

Increased attention to disability

Negative perceptions of physical disability were, to an extent, altered during the Intifada, the mass insurrection among Palestinians, which began in 1987, and which was symbolised by young Palestinian boys throwing stones at Israeli soldiers. Retaliation by the Israeli military to the Palestinian uprising caused a sudden, huge increase in the number of disabled people. The group most affected were younger adult men, who mainly suffered physical disabilities, with some cognitive impairments due to head injury. The immediate consequence was that, while disability had previously carried a stigma, it now became heroic: a sign of active resistance to the occupation. A source of shame had been transformed into a badge of honour.

The subsequent spread and development of services for people with physical disabilities in the region can be seen as a direct result of the emergence of the 'Intifada veterans'. Disability had become a political issue; service-provision and care for the disabled suddenly achieved a high profile. The focus remained pre-eminently one of emergency medical intervention, and clinical rehabilitation, exemplified by the establishment of the Abu Raya Centre in Ramallah, which was set up specifically to meet the medical needs of those injured in the Intifada.

In the aftermath of the 1948 Arab-Israeli war, UNRWA (United Nations Relief and Works Agency, a special body set up to care for the needs of Palestinian refugees in the region) and other similar charitable services were focused on emergency relief rather than long-term sustainable development. Together with the growth of large foreign-funded residential institutions providing care for the disabled, in areas such as Bethlehem, this has served to overemphasise relief and institutional care, at the expense of looking at disability as a rights issue. Charitable endeavours are a long-established means of foreign help to the people of this land.

Disability as a gender issue

As stated above, the high profile given to disabled people as a result of the Intifada had inevitably meant a focus on the physical injuries of young men. Disability was conceptualised as a martyrdom — young men cut down in their prime, forced to live out their lives in wheelchairs and unable to assume their expected social roles. The only other area focused on as a result of the Intifada was the needs of children disabled by war-related injuries. There was little or no development in other fields. This focus deflected the disability debate away not only from women, who also suffered during the Intifada, but also against those with congenital or non-physical impairments. Even today, there are no specialised services for adults with learning difficulties, and mental-health provision remains patchy and woefully inadequate.

Building a movement

It can be seen from the above that the status of disabled people in Palestine, post-Intifada, has not significantly improved. The honorific status accorded to the 'martyrs' has not automatically translated into an improved quality of life for all disabled citizens of the West Bank and Gaza.

In 1991, the General Union of Disabled Palestinians was formed as a pressure group bringing together disabled people, regardless of form of impairment or its cause. The organisation now has ten branches, and close to 4,000 members, in the West Bank. The organisation is the only non-service agency that effectively includes Intifada veterans and those with congenital disabilities. One of the problems facing the Union is the widespread narrowness of definition as to what constitutes disability. In Arabic, the word 'mua'qeen' denotes people with physical and sensory impairments. There is no concept with the scope to include other forms of impairment as well. The narrow focus on disabled war veterans compounds this problem.

Disability movements in the West have tended to focus on human rights as a way of raising awareness; and this approach groups together both physical and intellectual impairments under the heading of 'disability'. Palestinian society is subject to a widespread dissemination of Western attitudes and ideas as it continues to develop in the light of the Oslo agreements towards statehood. The social model of disablement (as opposed to the medical paradigm of disability) is gaining in popularity, and this is seen as the way in which the issue of discrimination is introduced to the disability debate.

From institutional to community care

The importance of community-based rehabilitation in transforming the lives of disabled people cannot be minimised. A community-based rehabilitation (CBR) programme was set up by UNRWA in the early 1980s, working with political committees, usually from the Fatteh party, which is the political wing of the Palestinian Liberation Organisation (PLO). These committees aimed through their work to promote community awareness and activity on the issues affecting disabled people, and to promote integration for disabled people at the community level. In 1990, a consortium of 14 NGOs also focused on community rehabilitation, while working in a very different way: through a process of needs identification, individual referrals, and only then the setting up of local committees to develop community participation.

Both these schemes are a move away from the institutional paradigm so common to aid programmes prior to the formulation of the CBR concept by the World Health Organisation Expert Committees on Disability Prevention and Rehabilitation, in 1981. UNRWA's strategy made use of the organisation of political factions to create community networks during the Intifada; the only strategy available at that time. In comparison, the newer CBR model used by the NGO consortium, implemented after the Intifada, was able to draw on a wider variety of sources for sustainable development, and could thus operate beyond the political spectrum.

However, while the CBR programmes have been extremely important for disabled people, it should be recognised that these programmes have concentrated more on individual 'interventionist' approaches, than on the creation of community channels for authentic social integration. The work is also primarily focused on children, both male and female. For example, in the village of Silwad, an eight-year-old girl, Samar, with mild learning difficulties and a speech impairment, was accepted into a mainstream kindergarten. Her mother recognises the beneficial role of the intervention in her daughter's life:

Before CBR's intervention, my kid always lived behind closed doors. She was isolated and had no discipline. Now she's much better-behaved, she goes out and tells us where she's going. She's also much more responsive.... Before going to the kindergarten, the other kids called her names, maybe they were afraid of her. Now she's their friend and they call her by her name. She's now a peer and not the butt of their jokes.

However, Samar's mother observed the pitfalls inherent in an intervention which depended too much on the involvement of outsiders, rather than being organically 'grown' by the community itself:

In the beginning, they [the CBR workers] were very enthusiastic and caring. But when my kid was kicked out of the kindergarten, they already had disappeared abruptly. There was no follow-up when I needed it.

If CBR activities are set up by a community, or a part of it, this is a signal that change to social attitudes surrounding disability is already under way. Remaining prejudice is likely to be easier to challenge. However, if the activity is designed and instigated by an external actor, the range of changes which need to come about — including attitudinal change — may be limited, and the activity may fail. For example, a mother with three children with multiple disabilities caused by cerebral palsy was taught home physiotherapy techniques by a CBR worker, as a result of which all three children are now able to walk unassisted. They don't go out of the house, because others view them with pity and disgust. Their sister, 16 years old, and not herself disabled, says:

It's a pity the CBR workers couldn't work on [my brothers' and sister's] brains as well as their legs; when they walk around, they damage everything in the home. People call my house, the 'home of the handicapped'. People are really negative, and CBR didn't change any attitudes; if people can feel it in their bones, then attitudes will change. I wish the community could love disabled people and not pity them; the CBR staff need to work compassionately rather than mechanically.

The same 16-year-old girl also identifies the gender issues associated with her disabled sister, and the fact that she herself is 'tainted' by association with disabled siblings, which damages her marriage prospects:

people say you shouldn't marry any girls from the family. When a would-be husband comes to see me and sees my sister and brothers, he scarpers. My Dad is OK about my brothers, but he really resents my sister.

It is clear from this anecdotal evidence that CBR programmes are effective in promoting sustainable home-grown intervention techniques, for example, physiotherapy and house adaptations, but less successful in creating the necessary community participation required for social awareness-raising.

Institutional responses to 'double discrimination'

There is a parallel between the emergence of the women's movement in Palestine and the disability movement. Both were created by exceptional political and social circumstances; both had a politicised (i.e. factional) structure; and, it can be argued, both movements have lost impetus since the end of the Intifada and the founding of the Palestinian Authority. Positive views surrounding disabled people currently spring from a revolutionary ethos; the challenge for groups such as the General Union of Disabled Palestinians is to sustain this impetus ensuring that all disabled Palestinians can share in the fruits of these endeavours.

In comparison, the Intifada permitted a strong Palestine women's movement to develop, partly as a result of the osmosis of Western liberal ideas, and an accompanying weakening of traditional social roles during the austerities of the time. A variety of women's action committees were created, to lobby for the promotion of women's rights across the whole spectrum of social roles. These committees and NGOs were built, as most organisations were at that time, on political factional structures. However, since the end of the Intifada, the women's movement has suffered as the secularisation process slows down.

Conclusion

The status of disabled women is gradually altering in Palestine. It is now not unheard of for a physically disabled woman to marry an able-bodied man. Disabled people are, perhaps, freer to marry out of personal choice than their non-disabled peers, who are more likely to submit to an arranged marriage. The ethos surrounding marriage allows disabled people more independence in those cases where marriage is not ruled out entirely. It should be stressed, however, that this is generally the case only for women with physical or sensory impairments; other types of disability do not necessarily produce this kind of freedom. In Gaza, for instance, in 1995, a woman with learning disabilities was raped by a gang of youths. She was subsequently murdered by her brother to alleviate the shame on the family.

These issues are recognised by the General Union of Disabled Palestinians as part of the so-called 'double discrimination' caused by gender-based and disability-based subordination. The management of the General Union of Disabled Palestinians consists of both disabled men and women. However, the status of women is an unresolved issue in Palestinian society as a whole; it is unlikely that the prevailing medical model of thinking about disablement and disability can hope to effect a social shift in attitude, without an accompanying change in perception of a range of issues surrounding equal opportunities.

Western gender and disability models are of limited use in that they cannot be imported wholesale to a new cultural environment without some adjustment over time. It is, perhaps, too early to speculate about how these issues will fit into the cultural and political context of an evolving Palestinian state. Initiatives like the General Union of Disabled Palestinians demonstrate the need felt by disabled men and women for far-reaching social change, but divisions within society hamper any attempt to embark on the long process of creating an atmosphere where equal opportunities can flourish.

Leila Atshan is a Lecturer and Trainer in Psycho-Social Issues at Bir Zeit University and YMCA, Jerusalem.

Facing the backlash:
one woman's experience in Yemen

Suad Ramadan

The situation of disabled persons in Yemen remains difficult; despite laws and decrees promulgated during the past six years relating to the creation of a special government fund for disabled persons, very few disabled persons have directly benefited from these laws.

Yemen is a very poor country: almost 30 per cent of the rural population lives in absolute poverty. There is therefore little chance that disabled people's needs can be met. For example, at a time when a minimum monthly salary is no more than 4000 Yemeni Rials (equivalent to £19 sterling), a basic second-hand wheelchair in poor condition can be bought at about 20-25000 Yemeni Rials (equivalent to £90–£115), thus restricting wheelchair use to the privileged. Basic rehabilitation services for the disabled are almost totally unavailable. About 69 per cent of people live in rural areas, where social services are almost non-existent. There is virtually no provision of disabled access to buildings, with the exception of a very few university premises, thus denying disabled people access to education and the work place. For those who suffer from multiple disabilities (the most common being learning disability and polio), the situation is even worse.

The situation of women

It is difficult to be precise about the way disability affects women in particular; this is partly because, given the context described above, there are very few studies which have looked at disability and gender together. Even general statistical information is scanty: for example, the information included in the most recent UNDP *Human Development*

In Yemen, women take little part in public life. When YAPH set up a women's committee, there was opposition from male colleagues.

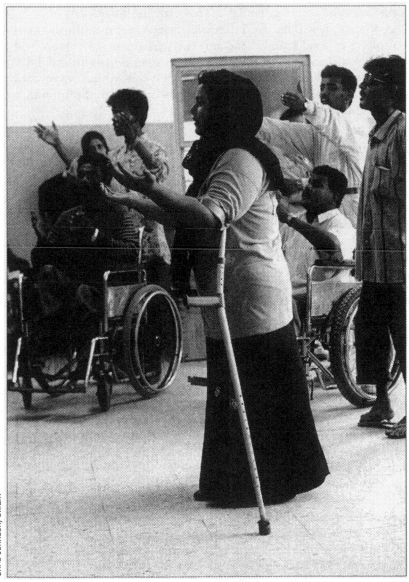

Chris Johnson/Oxfam

Report (1995) is incomplete, and most data on health, education, and economic activity are missing.

In general, women in Yemen are not much visible on the public scene. Their share of the adult labour force is 12–13 per cent; the female illiteracy rate is 91 per cent (compared to 51 per cent for men). It should be noted, however, that some progress has been reported in the past decade in the field of education and health, but the discrepancy between men and women remains quite substantial, as shown by the illiteracy rates.

In political life, there are 11 female council members in the local equivalents of municipalities, and only two parliamentary seats are held by women (of a total of 301 seats, ie.less that 1 per cent of total) (UNDP 1995). No portfolio is held by a woman, and only one woman has reached the level of Assistant Director general, while a limited number of women occupy middle-ranking and low-ranking jobs in the civil service.

The YAPH

A similar pattern can obviously be expected in the case of disabled women. In fact, any visitor to the Yemeni Association of Physically Handicapped (YAPH) centre in Sana'a will notice that the premises are almost entirely occupied by men, while a separate space is reserved for women. The association was created in 1988, and was the first formal organisation of physically disabled people in Yemen. YAPH is subsidised by the Yemeni government, and now attracts more than 400 disabled members of whom fewer than 10 per cent are women.

The mandate and objectives of the association have remained the same since it was set up: improving the general situation and well-being of disabled people, providing rehabilitation services and vocational training, and working towards the full social integration of disabled people. Activities have included providing rehabilitation equipment and financial assistance. There are no accurate data on the beneficiaries of these two services, and therefore it is difficult to tell how many were women. In common with many other associations of disabled people, there are no specific targets in respect of disabled women.

Initially, most of the association's activities involved holding meetings and gatherings within its premises and the participation in a number of sports events, notably the 1992 Paralympics in Barcelona. This was an important morale booster for the disabled athletes, who happened to be all men.

Campaigning and raising general awareness of disability issues became high on YAPH's agenda. Contacts were established with government officials, and many popular publications were produced and disseminated all over the country. Successful public fundraising campaigns were organised. In a relatively short time, the association was widely known by the public who became more aware of the plight of disabled persons. However, those who attended official ceremonies and meetings and went on fundraising events were all men.

Employment and vocational training

My involvement with the YAPH started in 1990. Part of my work was in providing assistance and support to the association in terms of programme planning, monitoring, and evaluation, in addition to budgeting and finances. I was also very much concerned with the female constituency of the association, which was largely invisible at that time, beyond the few vocational training courses offered by YAPH.

Vocational training was identified as a potential programme activity; this was encouraged by the availability of abundant international funding for such activities. The need for some activity to address the difficulty of unemployment among disabled women can be seen from the results of the job placement service offered by YAPH. The organisation succeeded in making more than 300 job placements possible, in both the private and public sectors; yet out of these, only ten were for women, eight of whom were employed by the association itself, as secretaries and vocational trainers.

Women attended vocational training courses in sewing, knitting, crochet, and other handicrafts. There was, however, no clear strategy as to the expected outcome in women's lives except gaining yet another useful 'feminine' skill. Unfortunately, very few, if any, possibilities for employment materialised as a result of these courses. In addition, many women were not even able to complete their training because of family pressure or inability to meet the cost of transport associated with the courses. Illiteracy amongst disabled women was a major problem. In this respect, the situation of disabled women in YAPH is similar to that of Yemeni women in general. Whereas most of the female members of YAPH are illiterate, the same is not true of their male colleagues, due to the fact that women are far less likely than men to receive education. This obviously makes women less eligible for any form of employment.

However, despite the limitations of the sewing and knitting classes, these still attracted a number of disabled women who saw in them the possibility of socialising outside their homes. From these courses came the idea of setting up a special women's committee. The purpose was to provide a free and safe space for disabled women to express themselves and to think of what sort of association they wanted. At the same time, other international donors were pressing the association 'to set up more women's projects' for which funding was readily available.

The development of the YAPH Women's Committee

The YAPH steering committee was composed of men only; due to cultural constraints, it was difficult for women to share the same public space as men. In fact, I felt that whenever men were present, the female trainees were intimidated and I could not have an open discussion with any of them. Jammalah, a disabled women and a member of the association, struck me as being the most confident. Her family had initially refused to allow her to join the association, but she persisted, and decided to challenge them despite any possible consequence. She therefore understood the difficulties that disabled women were going through, both at home and in the association.

Within YAPH, there was quite a lot of internal resistance to the idea of a separate women's committee. 'What is the point?' many asked. A women's committee was finally formed in 1992, and was headed by Jammalah, who was more vocal and better educated than the other four members. In my capacity as project officer for Oxfam, which was funding the YAPH, I worked closely with the women's committee, helping them to identify their role within the association. In addition to creating new projects for disabled women, the committee was also committed to securing better women's representation on the main YAPH steering committee.

Jammalah was a candidate for a place on the steering committee in 1993, and was elected by the general assembly. She was appointed as the person responsible for public relations within the steering committee, in addition to her role as the head of the women's committee. Oxfam saw in Jammalah a potentially important 'change agent' within the association, and we decided to invest further in working with her and in building her capacity.

My time with YAPH became largely taken up by discussions with the committee, and particularly with Jammalah. Together, we continuously searched for opportunities for training and capacity-building. The Oxfam Office procured numerous useful Arabic publications from elsewhere in the region, particularly from Lebanon, and organised visits by Jammalah and her women colleagues to disability groups in that country.

Jammalah's experience

In her role as YAPH Public Relations Officer, Jammalah gained a high profile with donor agencies, government officials, and other associations.

Her opinion on disability issues was trusted, and she had gained quite a lot of credibility as a result of her hard work in improving the situation of the association and further developing the women's committee. But the increase in her popularity within and outside the association, and the development of her network of relationships, caused increasing resentment among her male colleagues.

During that period came the preparations for the UN Fourth Conference on Women, in Beijing. As Oxfam Project Officer, I had invited Jammalah to participate in this international event, to encourage her to take part in the general debate on women. Jammalah and I attended a number of national preparatory meetings and workshops which took place in Yemen. Upon our return from Beijing, we noticed that the resentment within the steering committee had built up even further. Jammalah was relieved of her duties within the committee, despite protests from other women in the association. It was difficult for them to object too strongly; they were employed by YAPH, and feared losing their jobs. Although I and other agency staff attempted to mediate, our interventions were not welcomed by the committee.

Shortly after this, Jammalah was offered a post within the Ministry of Social Affairs, with whom she had worked on several occasions as a member of YAPH. She is one of the very few women who were able to become civil servants and certainly the only disabled woman.

Achievements of the women's committee

Throughout its existence, the women's committee was extremely active in reaching out to more women, encouraging families to break the isolation of disabled women, and attracting more and more female members to the association. In addition, the committee became involved in activities organised by women's associations in Yemen, who had never thought of integrating disabled women within their mandate and activities. Regional networking with other disabled groups, particularly their women's section, was also pursued by the committee, and they helped to prepare the Yemen National Report to Beijing.

The women's committee operated in difficult circumstances and had to overcome some resistance from their male colleagues. Jammalah's departure had a tremendous impact on the morale and work of the women's committee. Although it had been agreed that a mixed delegation should be sent on any exchange trips to other countries of the region, in fact the YAPH delegation sent to Lebanon in late 1995 was exclusively composed of men.

At this point, it is unclear how the women's committee will recover its impetus. In fact, the women's committee tried to pursue its course but the steering committee limited its role to maintaining members' jobs as secretaries and sewing and knitting trainers.

Lessons to be learned

The strategy followed by Oxfam had some success but also had serious drawbacks. Whereas I believe that we were truly able to build up the capacity and commitment of an individual woman (in this case Jammalah) this has failed to help the other members of the women's committee, and did not enhance the general position of women within the association.

Resentment from male colleagues is only to be expected in such situations. However, we should have been able to avert an irreversible situation such as Jammalah's dismissal from the steering committee. In addition to causing great pain to all those involved and dealing a severe blow to the morale of other women committee members, this has jeopardised future work on gender issues with the association.

In future, we need to take seriously the fact that men may feel threatened by a strategy to promote the interests of women. It is important to work with men, to enable them to understand and deal with the resistance they feel, and to come to believe that women's rights are a matter of natural justice which they have an obligation to support.

As a Project Officer, I feel that in my position, further gender training is of the utmost necessity, and so is the need to be more engaged with women's issues and women's groups at the national and regional levels.

Finally, the time spent with the women's committee was invaluable in encouraging discussions and explorations of issues and ideas. This I believe is the strength of Oxfam's field involvement and is itself a mechanism for change and for learning.

Suad Ramadan has been working with Oxfam in Yemen since 1990.
She is Lebanese and lives in Yemen with her husband and child.
Suad studied at the Lebanese University and has been for the past
15 years involved in literacy and popular education of grassroots
women in Lebanon and Yemen.

Taking the world stage: disabled women at Beijing

Jahda Abu-Khalil

The UN Fourth Conference on Women held in Beijing in September 1995 was an important event in the process of setting the future direction of international issues related to women's rights and gender equity. Earlier UN conferences on women — Mexico 1975, Copenhagen 1980, and Nairobi 1985 — succeeded in placing the issue of women high on the agenda of the United Nations and national governments; but they did not include consideration of disability as a 'women's issue', or integrate the views of disabled women into the conference proceedings and results. Thus, decisions reached on policy and action did not truly represent the interests of all groups of women. Able-bodied women cannot voice the concerns and interests of disabled women, in international or any other events. By and large, the overwhelming majority of women's groups, and the women's movement as a whole, have not really integrated or even taken into consideration the issue of women with disabilities.

The importance of the Beijing Conference is that, unlike its predecessors, it was infiltrated by disabled women organised into groups having a clear agenda. However, the disabled lobby was mainly representing disabled women from the North. Disabled women from developing countries, including Middle Eastern countries, were not sufficiently well-organised to be able to participate effectively.

By the time the Beijing Conference took place, the international context for disabled women had changed: a number of organisations and coalitions of women with disabilities have been formed over the past decade, and many prepared for Beijing despite considerable challenges and difficulties. One of these was Disabled People International (DPI), a Canadian-based international coalition of people with disabilities, which prepared for almost three years before the conference, attending all five regional preparatory meetings, and contributing to debates which determined the ten points of critical concern to women highlighted in the Beijing Platform for Action. This participation was a difficult task, given that the organisation of these preparatory meetings was not conducive to participation by women with disabilities.

The Beijing experience

Approximately 200 women with disabilities participated in the Beijing Conference and the NGO Forum at Huairou. Many more disabled women were expected in China, but were not able to get to the conference due to inability to secure funding coupled with numerous logistical obstacles (DPI, personal conversation). Most of the 200 participants came from the West and North America, with very limited representation from developing countries.

Disabled women attending the official opening of the NGO conference in Beijing

Jahda Abu-Khalil/Oxfam

The representation of disabled women from the Middle East in the UN Fourth Conference on women was weak. In the case of Lebanon and the Middle East, only about ten disabled women participated. In addition, women's organisations from the region failed in general to address the specific interests and concerns of disabled women; many appeared to lack all understanding of what it means to be both female and disabled. For example, the efforts of a Lebanese disabled woman to integrate a specific clause related to women with disabilities in a region-wide press communiqué on Beijing were unsuccessful. Arab NGOs met during the conference to prepare a joint position-statement to be issued to represent their regional concerns. The co-ordinator of the meeting was a male representative of a Lebanese NGO. During this meeting, a member of the Lebanese Sitting Handicapped Association drew his attention to the fact that no mention whatsoever was made about women with disabilities. She pointed out that the number of such women was relatively high across the regions as a result of the number of recent armed conflicts. It was suggested that if she put something in writing, it could be incorporated into the final text, but this did not happen.

Disabled women in Beijing organising a sit-in to protest against the inaccessibility of the premises.

Jahda Abu-Khalil/Oxfam

The official conference was attended by fewer than 20 disabled women, mostly from Western countries, who were able to obtain the necessary accreditation. Disabled women lobbied for the adoption by official delegations of the Standard Rules of the Equalisation for Persons with Disabilities (paragraph 41 in the Platform for Action), abolishing 'negative stereotyping of women with disabilities by the media', and adopting other measures which ensure 'commitment to promote employment of women with disabilities' (Report on the Beijing 1995 Conference, by DPI programme officer Justin Kiwanuka). A round table was organised, which aimed among other things to produce recommendations for ensuring that subsequent UN women's conferences will be more friendly and accessible to women with disabilities.

The NGO Forum at Huairou was the focus of most disabled women's participation in Beijing. A number of disabled people's organisations, such DPI, the Federation for the Deaf, the women's committee of the World Blind Union, and others, formed a women and disability network. The network organised the International Symposium of Women with Disabilities, attended mostly by the 200 disabled women participants at the conference. This event provided an opportunity for disabled women to meet, share experiences and issues of common concerns, discuss the Beijing Draft Platform for Action, and agree on a common strategy for the participation of women with disabilities in the Beijing conference.

The practical barriers to full participation in Beijing were severe. At the NGO Forum, women with disabilities had to face many practical challenges to their full participation. To start with, the tent focusing on disability was located far away from all the other tents (it took me, an able-bodied person, more than two days to find the disability tent), and access to it by wheelchair users was made even more difficult because of the frequent heavy rain. There were very few accessible toilets, and the transportation shuttles were completely unusable by disabled people. In addition, many of the special workshops for disabled women were held in upper floors of buildings which did not have ramps and elevators. As a result, women with disabilities joined in a peaceful protest and demanded that their participation in the conference be made more effective through the elimination of architectural barriers. Some of their demands were met; in particular, the site of the disability tent was changed, to a more visible and accessible venue, and some of the disability workshops were moved to ground-floor locations.

Despite all these difficulties, the representative of Disabled People International in her post-Conference report stated that the Beijing Conference had been worthwhile for women with disabilities. But although many women's groups shared a sense that progress had been made at Beijing, and that in many respects the cause of women's advancement had been taken forward, the lives of poor women are unlikely to change as a direct result of the conference. Able-bodied and disabled women might well share the same doubt as to the positive benefits they are likely to reap from such international gatherings.

The aftermath of Beijing

After the Beijing conference, it is now up to the women with disabilities in the region to improve their position, organisation, and representation and assert their presence within the women's movement, and within the disability movement. It was very clear that the need in future is for concerted efforts to organise and pool resources, and to start a constructive dialogue, both with women's groups and with the male-dominated disability groups in the region.

While the inadequate representation of disabled women from the Middle East at Beijing is unfortunate, it reflects a reality of poor organisation and lack of integration and co-operation between women with disabilities and women's NGOs in the region. The majority of NGOs which focus on women in the Middle East region are charitable institutions, run by and for women, and lack a concrete feminist agenda. This is particularly true in the case of Lebanon, where the women's movement is very weak, and presents little challenge to the marginalisation of women's issues from the political agenda and the isolation of women from decision-making in general, and from the public sphere. In comparison, the Lebanese disability movement is fairly vibrant. While it has experienced organisational problems, which hinder its efforts and achievements, recent efforts to pool forces and resources and create local and regional networks of organisations of disabled people in the Middle East may resolve these problems.

However, more effort will be needed if the disability movement is to truly represent the situation and position of women with disabilities. In the absence of a specific organisation of disabled women, these women have to operate from within the general disability movement, and challenge the prevailing tendency to ignore or marginalise women's issues. For example, a committee of blind women was formed after the general World Blind Union meeting held in Amman, Jordan in October 1995. The new committee, which included blind women from Jordan, Lebanon, Palestine, and Morocco, was and continues to be headed by a man.

In the follow-up activities to Beijing organised by the mainstream women's organisations, there are no provisions for disabled women. The National Association for the Rights of Disabled Persons in Lebanon (NARD) is currently developing a strategy for linking up with the official follow-up committee, and that formed by NGOs, to ensure that disability is included in the follow-up agenda.

Jahda Abu-Khalil is the editorial secretary of 'Assda' al Mouakeen',
a newsletter specialised in disability issues published by the 'National
Association for the Rights of Disabled Persons in Lebanon'.
She has a degree in clinical psychology from the Lebanese University.

4

Conclusion:
making 'imperfect' women visible;
strategies for the future

This final chapter will focus on the different possible strategies for
ensuring the full participation of women with disabilities in the development process, and making them 'visible' in development interventions.
Women with disabilities need to be able to participate and represent
their constituency in national and international decision-making,
including within the 'disability movement'. They need to undertake
lobbying and advocacy, integrating a clear gender perspective, to
promote the full and equal rights of women with disabilities.

Summing up the problems

The case studies presented in this book illustrate different facets of
oppression suffered by disabled women, as distinct from disabled men.
Though these gender-related issues raised in the case studies are in
many cases similar to issues familiar to able-bodied and disabled
women alike, disability acts to further increase the vulnerability of
women and reinforce their subordinate position in society.

We have noted that disabled women's access to resources differs from
individual to individual, and depends very much on the perceptions of
the decision-maker in the household as to the life-chances of the disabled
person. The life-chances of women and men are perceived very differently, and the effects of decision-making based on this criterion were
clearly demonstrated by the different treatment of male and female
children with disability within the same household described in the case
studies. The Youth Association for the Blind has reported that whereas a

blind girl was refused access to a special school for the blind, her parents saw no objections for her blind brother to attend the same school. This is not an isolated case; the impact of such a decision on the future of both children cannot be overemphasised; the life-chances of women are restricted by a vicious circle of negative perceptions leading to restricted or no educational opportunities for women.

As we have seen, not only does disability undermine women's opportunities in public life, in education and employment, much more than in the case of men; it also profoundly affects women's chances of a 'normal' life in the private sphere. Men with disabilities commonly marry — often an able-bodied woman, who subsequently serves as a lifetime carer. Such disabled men are able to maintain a family and lead a 'quasi-normal' life. In comparison, women with disabilities, unless they enjoy a degree of personal material wealth, would be unlikely to look forward to similar opportunities for marriage and family life. The alternative of an independent future is, of course, already closed to poor women, because of their lack of education and employment options.

Gender and disability are thus development issues: of the women with disabilities who were interviewed for this book, particularly in the course of the research study reported on in chapter 2, those who suc-ceeded (meaning here those who went to school, found jobs, developed and maintained friendships, and had an intimate relationship with a partner at some stage during their life) were invariably those women who were financially better-off. Often, they were supported by a male member of the household; in particular by their father. As this book notes, in discussions, such successful women tended to dismiss gender as a root cause of discrimination against them, stressing that it is their disability alone which is the source of all ills.

In short, poor women with disabilities are among the most disad-vantaged in our societies, and have very few opportunities in life to look forward to. Since very few resources are made available to them early on in life, they will be unable to break the vicious circle of dependency, isolation, and poverty. Our well-established patriarchal system means that there are persistent inequalities not only between able-bodied people and disabled people, but between women and men with disabilities.

The experience of Joce, recounted by Sister Sonia Samra, the director of the Bayt al Atfal Centre for Children with Learning Disabilities, is a powerful illustration of all these points:

We met Joce when she was eight years old, and was referred to our centre by a welfare institution. She had been placed in an orphanage after the death of her mother when she was only six. She came from a large family, and used to live in a very poor urban area, in one of the suburbs of Beirut. Joce was a pleasant little girl who showed signs of a moderate learning disability, which could have been made worse by a childhood spent in a poor and deprived environment. In 1990, our centre was badly hit by mortar shells and we had to close and send the children back to their families. Joce was then 13 years old.She went back to live with her father, who had abandoned her to the orphanage when she was a small child. She was a burden to him: what was he supposed to do with a vulnerable teenager?

Sister Sonia recounts the experience of Joce

We lost contact with Joce; we had no idea of how she was surviving in an environment where there are no laws or social support systems to protect her. When we saw her, two years later, she was pregnant, having been raped by a delinquent, a minor, living in her area. The reaction of her father was very violent, although Joce had received inadequate support, and lacked the strength, both mental and physical, to protect herself from any form of abuse.

Despite her problems, Joce insisted on keeping the baby. She was sent to a 'maison de re-education', for three months. She claimed her child back from the institution where he had been placed, determined to bring him up herself.

We tried very hard to initiate judicial proceedings against the rapist, and to ensure that Joce and her child claimed at least some minimum rights. However, Joce never revealed the identity of the man who raped her: she was too terrified. She cannot be blamed; nobody will protect her if he attacks her again. Disabled, poor, lacking any support from a male family member, she is an easy victim of any unscrupulous man. At the moment, she has no way of making a living for herself and her baby, and lives on handouts. She has no family support, and because her child is illegitimate, will always suffer from social stigma. Perhaps the worst thing of all is that she may well be raped again in future.

Patriarchy and the disability movement

The articles in this book have shown that male domination is a feature of the disability movement; how could it be otherwise when all our organisations spring from the cultures in which we are brought up to believe that male domination is the norm? Thus, many of the manifestations of male domination are ignored as they are seen as 'natural'. Nada Azzaz lives in Tripoli, and is blind. She is a founding member of the Friends of the Handicapped Association, and told us of an experience she had which shows the extent of male domination within the family:

The Friends of the Handicapped Association was created in 1986 by a group of disabled and able-bodied men and women. We founded a women's committee in 1994. We wanted more women to become members, and wanted to mobilise more grassroots women. We did not propose anything radical. My women colleagues and I went on home visits to find out more about the disabled women with whom we were working. We invited them to attend informal gatherings to discuss anything they were concerned about. For many, it was almost the first time that they had gone out of their houses on their own, and were given the opportunity to speak about their problems. Women came and talked about their lives, their childhood, their difficulties with their families, and with the outside world. After a few meetings, we missed one of the women. She had suddenly stopped coming. I was puzzled, because she had seemed to enjoy the meetings. So I went to see her;

perhaps she was ill or something. I was greeted rudely, and almost thrown out of her house When I was finally able to see her, I discovered that her brother had broken both her crutches to prevent her coming to our meetings. It was quite an effective deterrent.

Despite the high-minded aims of the disability movement to promote the rights of disabled people, and the increasing effectiveness of its advocacy and lobbying strategies, the movement — in common with government structures and other NGOs and national movements — does not necessarily challenge the existing male-dominated elites who make decisions in all these institutions.

Articles here have discussed the lack of representation of women within the leadership of the disability movement; the relative unawareness of gender issues as a determinant of life choices; and the overwhelmingly high proportion of male beneficiaries of rehabilitation services. These issues were reported by all the disabled women interviewed for this book.

Support from funding agencies often effectively reinforces such inequalities; disability is seen as a 'homogenous' and 'sexless' issue, thus failing to challenge gender-blind assumptions. Although many disabled men are able to enjoy sexual relations and a parental role, disabled women are almost always denied either of these fundamental human experiences. The story of a Lebanese woman dentist, married to a doctor, illustrates this point; when she suddenly became disabled, not only did her husband divorce her, but she was denied custody of her son, and only allowed to care for her daughter until the legal age (eight years old) when the child had to be handed over to her father.

Failing to acknowledge the fact that issues of gender discrimination strongly permeate, and ultimately determine, our attitudes towards disabled women and men inevitably results in collusion, either conscious or unconscious, on the part of individuals and organisations, with a patriarchal system which acts to keep women in an inferior position. Projects falling under the general aim of 'social integration' will only achieve partial integration since disabled men are better equipped to challenge and break down barriers and obstructive attitudes, stereotypes, and prejudices. Supporting the cause of women with disabilities requires us to review and challenge comfortable assumptions about disabled persons and the disability movement, and to be willing to put in place gender-specific strategies to address the particular needs and problems of disabled women.

Strategies for action

Most of the strategies outlined in this section were inspired by the experiences of disability groups in the Middle East and interviews with women with disabilities who are active within the disability movement.

Forming feminist organisations

One strategy is for women with disabilities to re-organise in women-only structures, so that they can address gender-specific issues and the resulting oppression of disabled women. In women-only organisations, the point of view of women is seen as natural and they no longer have to struggle to be heard.

Looking beyond basic needs

In devising strategies to bring about effective change, we need to over-come the temptation to design interventions which are limited to meeting only the immediate, short-term needs of people with disabilities.

Challenging sexism within the disability movement

As we have stated, the experience of disabled people in our societies and organisations is a microcosm of the wider development process within the external environment. This book shows that it is also a clear example of gender-blind development. In the first chapter, we explored the way in which resistance and opposition to gender are manifested both within and outside the disability movement. Gender and development workers and activists need to feel comfortable in challenging disability groups in order to bring about the needed awareness and consciousness of gender issues in disabilities. It is reasonable to expect resistance in different forms, from both men and women with disabilities, as well as from those who work alongside them.

'Gendering' the agenda of the disability movement

We have noticed that groups and associations of people with disabilities often feel uneasy about the issue of gender. This seems to be because of a combina-tion of a negative attitude towards gender equality with an ignorance about the relation of gender to development and poverty. The consequence is an unwillingness to address gender issues, and an assertion that gender is either not relevant to disability, or not a priority, especially when funds are limited.

It has proved to be extremely challenging in such situations to introduce gender into an otherwise gender-blind agenda. However, these challenges are familiar from other contexts, and are certainly not peculiar to the disability movement. We can learn from the experience of introducing, mainstreaming, and supporting gender in other development fields. In addition to developing mechanisms which allow lessons and experiences to be distilled and absorbed, such tools as Oxfam (UK) gender policy are effective for mainstreaming gender issues in the agenda of disability groups. Oxfam's gender policy has been used both to introduce a discussion of gender issues and as a possible model of how political will can be translated into action. This process carries with it, however, the risk of gender being seen as a concept introduced and imposed by an external agency. This is of particular significance given the perceived inequality of power within the relationship of funding agencies with local NGOs and groups.

Investing in research and communication

While research on disability per se is abundant, there has so far been little research carried out in relation to the specific issues affecting women with disabilities. According to many women with disabilities, this is probably due to the fact that disability, rather than the gender dimension, is seen as the main concern. For many able-bodied and disabled individuals, disability causes equal suffering, and creates equal problems for men and for women. In fact, the only perceived difference occasionally mentioned is in relation to marriage, as the number of married men with disabilities is visibly higher than amongst women with disabilities.

Preparations leading to the UN Fourth Conference on Women which was held in Beijing in September 1996 provided an opportunity for reflection and small-scale empirical studies on gender differences in the experience of disability. Examples of such studies are presented in this book. Groups of disabled persons involved in lobbying and advocacy have noted that the better equipped they were with studies and research to back up their advocacy agenda, the better and stronger their positions were, and the higher their chances of success. It is therefore reasonable to draw a parallel in the case of women and disability and invest in research in this particular field.

Research and communication on gender and disability are not only of benefit in terms of raising the profile of the issues but also in planning and implementing programmes. The Youth Association for the Blind has reported that, following its in-depth study of six blind women of South Lebanon, it was able to undertake an informed review and evaluation of the adequacy of its programme in meeting the specific needs and concerns of blind women.

Mainstreaming disability in the women's movement

During a workshop organised by the National Association for the Rights of Disabled Persons on 'Women with Disabilities towards the year 2000' (Beirut, April 96), Dr. Fahmyah Charafeddine, an able-bodied sociologist and activist, gave a presentation on 'Disabled Women and Civil Society' in which she drew attention to the fact that the women's movement in Lebanon has so far failed to absorb and integrate issues of disability; and that weaknesses within the women's movement limits the advancement of women with disabilities. Very few women's groups and women activists have so far considered that their demands may be inadequate to change the situation and position of disabled women. WILDAF (Women in Law and Development in Africa) is one of the few women's groups who have begun to give due attention to disability. During a one-day workshop held in Kadoma in November 1995 to look at women's legal problems, with particular focus on disabled women, WILDAF acknowledged that 'women with disabilities sometimes face problems which are peculiar to them'. Some of the main examples given were specific problems with regard to health issues, such as the inaccessibility of health services to disabled women, and the sterilisation of women with disabilities. The final recommendations from the workshop included specific points related to women with disabilities.

Mainstreaming disability within the women's movement was said by Sylvana Lakkis, president of the Lebanese Sitting Handicapped Association, to be the priority strategy to be pursued by the Association in order to further the cause of women with disabilities and contribute to the diversity and strength of the women's movement.

Supporting linkages between women with disabilities

There are very few structures available to allow women with disabilities to communicate experiences, and join forces to overcome their marginalisation and invisibility. Jahda Abou-Khalil of the National Association for the Rights of Disabled Persons who participated in the Beijing Conference said that the isolation of women with disabilities was obvious not only at the regional level but also within each country delegation. According to her, this lack of communication and collective preparation led, at least in the case of the Middle East delegation, to an absence from the lobbying agenda of issues raised by women with disabilities, and therefore to a failure to represent their concerns at a major international forum.

The women's movement and the disability movement have both gained strength and increased visibility as a result of forming links and alliances within and across countries. Women with disabilities need to be supported in their efforts to create and maintain linkages and permanent communication channels and networks either internationally, regionally or within countries.

Gender training and capacity building

Training and capacity building for work on gender issues is still at a preliminary stage in the Middle East. However, the impetus to intensify this work was encouraged by the preparations leading to the Beijing Conference and further reinforced by what are referred to as 'the Beijing follow-up processes'. However, since disability groups have been less involved in these processes, they have been less exposed to gender training and capacity building. None of the disability groups and activists with whom Oxfam (UKI) is involved in the Middle East have gone through a systematic gender training programme. The need for such training is now regarded as a priority by a number of association leaders, who see it as a necessity to improve their organisations' understanding, analysis, vision, and programme response.

Empowering women with disabilities

Disability may not necessarily represent a binding force between men and women with disabilities. In fact gender inequalities remain unaffected or even exacerbated by disability. A group discussion held with women and men activists from the Lebanese Sitting Handicapped Association has shown that men with disabilities clearly felt and believed in their superiority over women with disabilities.

A disabled Yemeni woman member of the Yemeni Association of the Physically Handicapped said during an interview in preparation for this book that she and her female colleagues would like to see more women in decision-making positions in her association. According to her, associations such as hers should be more serious in promoting the interests of disabled women, and should avoid 'window dressing tactics' to please external funding agencies. This she believes can only come about when disabled women are strong enough to become part of the leadership of groups and associations of disabled persons rather than mere recipients of aid, administered without prior consultation with them. The present situation, she adds, is one which makes disabled women feel weak and disadvantaged in comparison to their male colleagues.

More examples can be found to illustrate attitudes within the disability movement which disempower disabled women and increase their vulnerability. It is therefore essential to identify, support, and empower individual disabled women within a disability group or association. Support to these women may take the form of training and capacity building, and facilitating linkages with women's groups. However, focusing on individuals in this way may be misinterpreted as encouraging divisions within groups which would otherwise be homogeneous and harmonious. In fact, groups are rarely homogeneous as needs and aspirations are largely determined by gender as well as other factors of social differentiation.

Interventions which are gender-blind are not only those which ignore or discriminate against women with disabilities. Interventions intended to target both men and women with disabilities can be equally damaging if they fail to recognise that the ability to benefit from a given service or project is determined not only by the availability of that service but even more by people's earlier experience of disability and the impact of gender differences in access to resources in the earlier stages of life. A vivid example of this is a credit scheme implemented since 1991 by the Friends of the Handicapped in North Lebanon. Although not in the least intending to discriminate against women with disabilities, the scheme ended up by serving far more disabled men than women. An analysis of the impact of the scheme revealed that although the fund was advertised and made available to all persons with disability meeting certain criteria for eligibility, only those who were sufficiently educated, were mobile, and had some earlier work experience were able to take advantage of it. The overwhelming majority of these happened to be men!

The cause of women with disabilities will not progress unaided. A general improvement in the lives of disabled persons and the recognition of their fundamental rights will not necessarily affect women and men equally, nor bring about a positive and long-lasting change in the lives of women with disabilities. Given the differential access to and control over resources which as we have seen prevails between women and men with disabilities, we can assume that the extent and impact of poverty among women with disabilities is potentially greater. Therefore, gender-blind interventions will only serve to reinforce existing inequalities between women and men with disabilities.

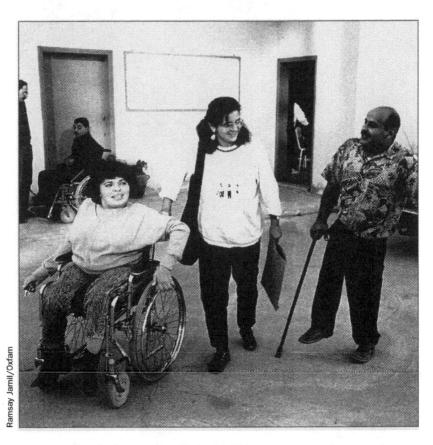

Sylvana Lakkis and Mohammed Ali, both LHSA committee members, set off to a preparatory meeting for the Beijing conference with Lina Abu-Habib.

Resources

compiled by Georgia Gili

Further reading

Abu-Habib L, *Women And Disability Don't Mix:*
Double Discrimination And Disabled Women's Rights in Sweetman C, (ed.),
Gender And Development: Women And Rights, pp. 49–53, Vol. 3, No. 2,
Oxfam UK/Ireland, June 1995.
Argues that it is imperative to understand and address gender issues and
how they impact upon a person's experience of disability, in order to
develop a strategy for establishing and enforcing the human rights of
women and men with disabilities.

Awdeh M & al Hajj Ali A, *Focus On The Lives Of Disabled Women*
In Palestinian Society, Birzeit University, 1992.
Case histories of nine Palestinian disabled women. Attempts to identify
the differences in life opportunities and expectancies. Focuses on access
to resources, and how the political conflict has impacted on disabilities,
as determined by gender.

Begum N, *Disabled Women And The Feminist Agenda,* in *Feminist Review,*
pp. 70–84, No. 40, 1992.
Demonstrates how the concerns of disabled women are crucial to both
the disability rights and feminist movements. Gives emphasis to three
factors, vital to an understanding of the lives of women: gender roles,
self-image, and sexuality.

Boylan E, *Women And Disability,* Zed Books Ltd,
London & New Jersey, 1991.
A series of articles on a wide range of issues affecting women with disabilities. Includes suggestions for education and action, organisations, additional reading, and audio-visual materials.

DAA, *Disability Awareness In Action Newsletter,* No. 29,
Disability Awareness In Action, July 1995.
An edition devoted to the preparations for the NGO Forum and the Fourth United Nations Conference on Women. Includes the international disability NGOs' demands regarding the Platform for Action and the Forum and Conference.

DAA, *Disability Awareness In Action Newsletter,* No. 32, November 1995.
News from the Women's Committee of Disabled People's International about the United Nations Conference on Women and the NGO Forum.

Driedger D & Gray S, (ed.) *Imprinting Our Image: An International Anthology By Women With Disabilities,* Gynergy Books, Canada, 1995.
A collection of writings from 17 different countries, in which women with disabilities confront a world which has imposed false and constricting images upon them. For more information please contact: Lee Fleming, Marketing Manager, PO Box 2023, Charlottetown P.E.I, C1A 7N7 Canada. Tel: (902) 566-5750 Fax: (902) 566-4473.

DPI, *Vox Nostra,* pp. 18–21, Volume 1, No. 4, Disabled People's International, December 1994.
Information about DPI's Women's Committee and the preparations for the Fourth World Conference on Women.

DPI, *Vox Nostra: Disabled Europeans: Our Voice,* p. 13, DPI,
European Region, May 1995.
Details of the international symposium on issues of women with disabilities in preparation for the NGO Forum and Fourth U.N. World Conference on Women.

DPI, *Women And Disabilities,* DPI, 1987.
A paper presented at the regional experts' seminar to review achievements at the mid-point of the UN-Decade of Disabled Persons, Bangkok, Thailand, 1987. Available in English only. Available from Disabled People's International, 101-107 Evergreen Place, Winnipeg, Manitoba, Canada R3L 2T3. Tel: 204-287-8010 Fax: 204-287-8175, for $2 (postage and handling).

DPI Women's Committee, *DPI Women's Kit*, DPI, undated.
The women's resources kit is a source of information regarding the committee's mandate, objectives and achievements, as well as promoting awareness about disabled women's issues. Available in English only from DPI, please see address above.

ESCWA, United Nations Economic Commission For Western Asia, *Disabled Women In Eygpt*, unpublished paper for United Nations Conference, November 1994.
Copies available from Gender Team Library, Policy Department, Oxfam, Banbury Road, Oxford, UK, OX2 7DZ.
Tel: 01865- 312363. Fax: 01865-312600.

Hannaford S, *Living Outside Inside: A Disabled Woman's Experience. Towards A Social And Political Perspective.* Canterbury Press, Berkeley, California, USA, 1985.
A collection of essays, articles, and letters arising from one woman's experience of disability. Intended for a variety of readers, some pieces have a powerfully personal stance, while others are very much more academic and theoretical.

Hermans P. C, *Equal Treatment Of Men And Women In Social Security: An Overview*, International Social Security Association, in International Social Security Review, pp. 250–260, 41(3), (Geneva), 1988.
Surveys the outcome of research into the complaints of Dutch women's organisations about the unequal treatment of women in Dutch disability insurance legislation.

ILO, *Amman Jordan: Report Of The Workshop On The Development Of Policies And Programmes For Social And Vocational Rehabilitation For Disabled Women In The Middle East Region.* Report of the Workshop held in Amman, Jordan, ILO, 1987.
Recommends the development of legislation to encourage the employment of disabled women and to ensure their rights to medical, psychological, social, educational, and vocational rehabilitation services. Available in Arabic from the International Labour Organisation, Vocational Rehabilitation Branch, 4 Route des Morillons, CH-1211, Geneva, Switzerland.

ILO, *Dispelling The Shadows Of Neglect: A Survey On Women With Disabilities In Six Asian And Pacific Countries*, ILO, Geneva, 1989.
Demonstrates clearly the need for attitudinal change from the general public towards disabled women.

ILO, *Integration Of Persons With Disabilities: Information For Policy-Makers And Decision-Makers,* Rehabilitation Staff Training And Research Programme For Africa: Harare, Training For Integration And Participation Series, ILO, 1993.
A gender-sensitive approach to integrating people with disabilities into community planning and development. Defines integration and the ways to achieve it.

ILO, *No Application Form: Poems And Stories By Women With Disabilities From Southern Africa; A Glimpse Of The Lives Of Women With Disabilities: Report On A Study Of 150 Women With Disabilities In Gokwe And Harare,* ILO, Harare, 1993.
Looks at the lives and coping strategies of women with disabilities in one rural and one urban area of Zimbabwe.

Keith L, (ed.) *Mustn't Grumble: Writing By Disabled Women,* The Women's Press, London, 1994.
A collection of wide-ranging writings by disabled women.

Kojima Y, *Analytic Report On Socio-Vocational Integration Of Disabled Women In Japan: A National Research Project For The ILO; A Study On Disabled Women, Caregivers And Agencies, And Recommendations For Practical Actions To Promote Integration Of Disabled Women,* Tokyo Office Of Social Rehabilitation Research, ILO, 1988.
One of a series of regional surveys which aims to improve the social and employment conditions of disabled women. Reviews the current situation for disabled women and women carers of disabled people in relation to trends in rehabilitation in Japan.

Morris J, *Tyrannies Of Perfection,* in, Baird V, (ed.), *New Internationalist,* pp. 16–17, No. 223, 1992.
How the disability movement is confronting issues raised by abortion, euthanasia, and genetic engineering.

Morris J, *Pride Against Prejudice: Transforming Attitudes To Disability,* Women's Press, London, 1993.
Debates the nature of prejudice against disabled people and the emerging international disability movement.

Rodwell B, *Disabled Women: A Fighting Force,* in, Lloyd L & Meer S, (eds.), *SPEAK,* pp. 30–32, Johannesburg, 1991.
An interview with the deputy chairperson of Disabled People South Africa, who argues strongly that disability is a political issue.

Stance S, *Vocational Rehabilitation For Women With Disabilities*, ILO, Geneva, 1986.
A study of the double discrimination faced by disabled women. Reveals that disabled women are not being admitted to employment schemes designed for women or vocational rehabilitation programmes for disabled people. Contains a bibliography and literature review.

Stance S, *Vocational Training For Women With Disabilities*, in, *International Labour Review*, pp. 301–316, 126(3), May–June, ILO, Geneva, 1987.
Demonstrates that disabled women who work have limited access to the labour market because of the double disadvantage of being both disabled and women. Criticises the inadequacies of present rehabilitation systems and argues that more active measures are needed to tackle such discrimination.

Audio-Visual Resources

All In Your Head, Pearson J, (dir.), b/w, U-matic/VHS (6mins), 1991, UK.
Raises the profile of epilepsy and aims to challenge stereotypes about this 'invisible' disability. Available to hire from CineNova, 113 Roman Road, London E2 0QN, UK. Tel: 0181-981-6828. Fax: 0181-983-4441.

A One Way History, VHS (15mins), 1990, UK.
Looks at issues of race and disability from the point of view of four young women with learning disabilities. Supplied by 20th Century Vixen, 74 St. James's Drive, London SW17 7RR. Tel: 0171-682-0587.

A Prayer Before Birth, Duckworth J, (dir.), 16mm/VHS (20mins), 1991, UK.
A drama based on the director's experience of coming to terms with multiple sclerosis. Available to hire from CineNova, 113 Roman Road, London E2 0QN, UK. Tel: 0181-981-6828. Fax: 0181-983-4441.

For A Better Future And A Better Life: Women And Disability,
Lebanese Sitting Handicapped Association (LSHA), VHS, 1995.
How LSHA are employing a community based rehabilitation, (CBR), strategy to enable people with disabilities to mobilise local resources. LSHA place great importance on achieving attitudinal change especially towards disabled women, who are less likely than their male counterparts to find employment, and therefore consciously recruit women leaders to co-ordinate their projects. Copies are available on loan from the Gender Team, Policy Department, Oxfam, 274 Banbury Road, Oxford, OX2 7DZ, UK. Tel: 01865-312363. Fax: 01865-312600.

For Good, Booth C, (dir.), 16mm/VHS (45mins), 1979, UK.
Through the stories of Angie, Helen and Geoff, the film aims to provoke able-bodied audiences to examine their attitudes towards people with cerebral palsy. Available to hire from CineNova, 113 Roman Road, London E2 0QN, UK. Tel: 0181-981-6828. Fax: 0181-983-4441.

It's The Same World, UN, 16mm/VHS (20mins), 1981.
Created to mark the United Nations International Year Of Disabled Persons this film is a plea for full participation and equality for the disabled. Available in Arabic, English, French and Spanish from the United Nations Audio-Visual Promotion and Distribution Unit, Media Division, Department of Public Information, Room S-805B, United Nations, New York, NY 10017. Tel: (212) 963-6939. Fax: (212) 963-6869. E-mail: Sue-Ting-Len@un.org

Loss Of Heat, Deville N, (dir.), 16mm (20mins), 1994, UK.
A magical portrayal of epilepsy and love that illustrates the relationship between the carer and the cared for. Focusing on two parallel lesbian relationships this film reflects the reality of living with an 'invisible' disability. Available to hire from CineNova, 113 Roman Road, London E2 0QN, UK. Tel: 0181-981-6828. Fax: 0181-983-4441.

The Disabled Women's Theatre Project, VHS/U-matic (60mins), 1982, USA.
Explores and communicates the experience of disability through theatre in a dynamic series of performances. Available to hire from CineNova, 113 Roman Road, London E2 0QN, UK. Tel: 0181-981-6828. Fax: 0181-983-4441.

Warrior Marks, Pratibha P, (dir.) VHS, (54mins), 1993, UK.
Charts the journey of Alice Walker from California to England, Gambia and Senegal, meeting courageous and inspiring women who have survived to fight against the disabling practice of female genital mutilation. Available to hire from CineNova, 113 Roman Road, London E2 0QN, UK. Tel: 0181-981-6828. Fax: 0181-983-4441.

Organisations working in the field of gender and disability

Friends Of The Handicapped Association (FOH)
PO Box 670
Tripoli
Lebanon

Lebanese Sitting Handicapped Association (LSHA)
PO Box 100/4740
Beirut
Lebanon

National Association For The Rights Of Disabled Persons (NARD)
PO Box 113/5157
Beirut
Lebanon

Youth Association For The Blind (YAB)
PO Box 113/5487
Beirut
Lebanon

The four organisations listed above are unions or groups of disabled persons working in lobbying and advocacy as well as in regional and international networking around issues on disabled rights with specific focus on disabled women.

Rehabilitation Association For The Disabled (RAD)
c/o Oxfam Beirut Office
PO Box 113/5211
Beirut
Lebanon

Bayt Al Atfal Centre For Mentally Handicapped Children
c/o Sister Sonia Samra
PO Box 25
Kornet Shehwan Al-Metn
Lebanon

The two organisations listed above are involved in training and special education for mentally disabled people. They have specific programmes for women carers of disabled within the family and in institutions.

Disability Awareness In Action, (DAA), is an international public education campaign, established in 1992 to promote, support and coordinate national action by disabled people's own organisations and their allies. DAA can be contacted at:

DAA
11, Belgrave Road, London SW1V 1RB.
Tel: 0171-834-0477
Fax: 0171-821-9539
Minicom: 0171-821-9812

Formed in 1980/81, Disabled People's International, (DPI), is an international campaigning organisation and coordinating body for disabled people's organisations and networks. DPI's Women's Committee is a resource development vehicle for working with gender issues from within DPI structures. DPI can be contacted at:

DPI
101-107 Evergreen Place
Winnipeg
Manitoba
Canada R3L 2T3
Tel: 204-287-8010 Fax: 204-287-8175

Access to DPI's publications list and a list of other disability related web and gopher sites on the World Wide Web can be gained via: http://www.escape.ca/~dpi/publist.html
Please note that this page and all subsequent DPI pages will be provided in French and Spanish as well as English. Any questions, concerns or comments regarding this page can be e-mailed to: DPI@dpi.org
Other disability related resources on the web can be accessed via: http://fohnix.metronet.com/~thearc/misc/disInkin.html

Feminist Audio Books provide a library service of taped material, especially feminist and lesbian material, for blind, partially sighted and print impaired women and men. The material is on ordinary cassette tapes, available through the post. Contact FAB for a free catalogue.

Feminist Audio Books (FAB)
52-54 Featherstone Street
London EC1Y 8RT
UK
Tel: 0171-251 2908

Gemma aims to lessen the isolation of disabled lesbian and bisexual women of all ages by making the lesbian community, and society in general, more aware of their existence and needs. Gemma can supply information and speakers, workshop material and a list of publications. Please contact:

Gemma
BM Box 5700
London WC1N 3XX
UK

Mobility International USA is a non-profit making organisation dedicated to expanding equal opportunities for persons with disabilities in international education exchange, leadership development, disability rights training, travel and community service.

Mobility International USA (MIUSA)
PO Box 10767
Eugene, OR 97440
Tel: (541) 343-1284 (voice/tdd)
Fax: (541) 343-6812 E-mail: miusa@igc.apc.org

RADAR is a national organisation working with and for disabled people. RADAR campaigns for equal rights for disabled people and supports over 500 member groups locally and nationally in the UK. Offers information, advice and a database of organisations.

RADAR
12 City Forum
250 City Road
London EC1V 8AF
UK

Formed in 1994, SHE UK aims provide a forum for disabled women to discuss how disability has affected their sexual lives. SHE UK aims to build up a network of disabled women to become involved in conferences.

SHE UK
BM Box 5192
London WC1N 3XX
UK

WinVisible is a grassroots network of women from many different backgrounds, with visible and invisible disabilities who campaign for economic independent mobility and other resouces for intergrated living. As an England-based network, WinVisible are aware that the lives of people with disabilities are even harder in countries where there is no welfare. WinVisible support the fight for universal standards of rights and resources based on the needs of disabled people. Information and other materials are available on audio-tape. WinVisible can be contacted at:

WinVisible
Women With Visible And Invisible Disabilities
King's Cross Women's Centre
71 Tonbridge Street
London WC1H 9DZ
UK
Tel: 0171-837-7509 Voice and Minicom
Fax: 0171-833-4817

Printed in the USA
CPSIA information can be obtained
at www.ICGtesting.com
JSHW012043140824
68134JS00033B/3224